# ORDER OF THE ARROW HANDBOOK

## BOY SCOUTS OF AMERICA

1991 Printing
1990 Revision
Copyright 1989
Boy Scouts of America
Irving, Texas
ISBN 0-8395-5000-6
No. 5000 Printed in U.S.A.

# Contents

# ORDER OF THE ARROW
# PERSONAL RECORD

Name: _____

Street: _____

City, State: _____

## Ordeal Membership

Call-Out:    Date: _____

            Location: _____

Ceremony:    Date: _____

            Location: _____

Lodge: _____ # _____

## Brotherhood Membership

Ceremony:    Date: _____

            Location: _____

Lodge: _____ # _____

## Vigil Honor

Call-Out:    Date: _____

            Location: _____

Ceremony:    Date: _____

            Location: _____

Vigil Honor Indian Name: _____

English Translation: _____

Lodge: _____ # _____

## Offices Held:

_____
_____
_____
_____

## Section and National Events Attended:

_____
_____
_____
_____

# Foreword

For those readers who are new Arrowmen, welcome! This edition of the *Order of the Arrow Handbook* has been written especially for you, for you are the future of the Order.

To veteran members of the Order, you will find this edition helpful in many ways. While some sections and words will seem familiar, take note that much of what is contained between the covers of this handbook is important to all Arrowmen.

This handbook brings together the basic knowledge that all members will want to know. In addition, many topics have been expanded for clarity and emphasis.

This *Order of the Arrow Handbook* reflects the current policics concerning the organization of the Order of the Arrow lodge. Use this handbook as your guide.

# GUIDE FOR MEMBERS

# Purpose and Principles

You may recall that Meteu recounted the legend of the Lenni Lanape Indians during the final part of the Ordeal Ceremony. Among the things he said: "In a great and honored Order, into which can be admitted only those who unselfishly desire to serve others, there must be a lofty purpose. You were selected for membership in the Order because your fellow Scouts saw your sincerity and acceptance of the high ideals of the Scout Oath and Law."

As a member of the Order of the Arrow, you must fulfill the trust and confidence bestowed upon you by your fellow Scouts with this mighty purpose: The essence of our existence is that we must be those campers—Boy Scouts, Explorers, and Scouters—who best exemplify the Scout Oath and Law in our daily lives and by such conduct cause others to emulate our actions. We who bear the Obligation of the Order of the Arrow, mindful of our high tradition, ponder that which is our purpose, and do pledge ourselves to cheerful service.

## Purpose of the Order

*To recognize those campers—Scouts, Explorers, and Scouters—who best exemplify the Scout Oath and Law in their daily lives and by such recognition cause other campers to conduct themselves in such manner as to warrant recognition.*

*To develop and maintain camping traditions and spirit.*

*To promote Scout camping, which reaches its greatest effectiveness as a part of the unit's camping program, both year-round and in the summer camp, as directed by the camping committee of the council.*

*To crystallize the Scout habit of helpfulness into a life purpose of leadership in cheerful service to others.*

## Principles of the Order

You were inducted into the Order of the Arrow "not so much for what you have done, but for what you are expected to do." For in taking the Obligation of the Order, you promised, on your honor, "to be unselfish in service and devotion to the welfare of others."

This is not an easy pledge to fulfill, for there are few who live a life of cheerful service in our world. For some, the Order will be like a supernova, shining brilliantly for a brief time and soon crumbling to ashes. For others, the Order will kindle a flame of brotherhood, brighter than a thousand suns, lasting throughout eternity.

During your candidacy, you have impressed upon those fellow members who have lived closest to you the sincerity of your purpose to live in accordance with the high ideals of the Scout Promise. The judgment of your fellows can hardly have been mistaken.

Now the time to judge has come. You have entered our Brotherhood. The distinctive pocket emblem and sash are yours. Now you are to face another test, one administered and graded solely by yourself. Will you embrace the traditions and obligations of our Order?

Your election into our Order was indeed unique. There is no other organization in which members are elected by nonmembers. Any organization that inducts from the inside is prone to lose touch with society, but your election was based on the standards set by your fellow Scouts. Thus the Order, grounded in outdoor camping, will continue to be relevant to today's society.

# Camping and the Order

Camping is a method of Scouting, but camping is not Scouting's purpose. Scouting aims to build character, citizenship, and fitness. When Scouts go camping, this growth just seems to follow. Patrol and troop camping are models and a testing ground for life in society. In a small group, each member is dependent on the others. Each learns to accept responsibility and to exercise good judgment. Even a stubborn or selfish person finds himself interacting with others in helpful and supportive ways. Scouts who camp will sooner or later come face to face with practical applications of the Scout Oath and Law. Cheerfulness, trustworthiness, courtesy, helpfulness, and all the central virtues of Scouting are necessary in camp and in society. Life in the open is a natural teacher of these essential survival skills. Thus, we promote camping, and camping becomes more effective in achieving the aims of Scouting.

The principles of Scouting are central to any kind of successful camping. The Order of the Arrow arose in a Scout camp, and it keeps camping promotion as a major service. Arrowmen encourage Scouts to go camping. In camp we maintain the best traditions and the highest spirit.

9

## Order of the Arrow Obligation

I do hereby promise, on my honor as a Scout, that I will always and faithfully observe and preserve the traditions of the Order of the Arrow, Wimachtendienk, Wingolauchsik, Witahemui.

I will always regard the ties of brotherhood in the Order of the Arrow as lasting, and will seek to preserve a cheerful spirit, even in the midst of irksome tasks and weighty responsibilities, and will endeavor, so far as in my power lies, to be unselfish in service and devotion to the welfare of others.

(Sign your name.)

## The Obligation

Although our many service projects are valuable to Scouting, the main benefit is less obvious. The Order's primary concern is the individual, and the Order's function is to spread the spirit of brotherhood and cheerful service. You do the work of the Order in your home, your troop, and your school, as you keep the fire of the Scout Oath alive in words and deeds. More than anything else, your own example of cheerful service to others accomplishes the Order's aim.

The Obligation of the Order is one way we remind ourselves of our special duties. Memorize it just as you did the Scout Oath and Law. Remember the three principles of the Order, and you will easily learn it.

"Wimachtendienk, Wingolauchsik, Witahemui" means "the brotherhood of cheerful service" or "brotherhood, cheerfulness, and service," the three principles of the Order. Thus the second sentence of the Obligation is an explanation of the first.

Your actions in living the Obligation as a member of your troop fulfill the primary goals of the Order. As you read, you will see how you can promote camping and camping traditions in your troop, how you can help your fellow Scouts, and how you can participate in the activities of the Order. But remember the main work of the Order is done by you, usually alone and without praise or reward. "He alone is worthy to wear the Arrow who will continue faithfully to serve his fellow man."

When Dr. Goodman and his Treasure Island camp staff started the Order in 1915, they realized that the Scouts who were to be chosen to set the example in their troops would need further encouragement and inspiration if they were to fulfill their role in Scouting. They devised the Ordeal to give the new Arrowmen this inspiration in the form of an experience involving the ideals they were to follow:

• Eat you nothing but the scant food you'll be given. Learn by fasting, sacrifice, and self-denial to subordinate personal desires to the spirit's higher purpose.

• Your directions are the whispers, urgings, promptings, deep within your hearts and spirits. Therefore, till you take the Obligation, strictly keep a pledge of silence.

• Spend the day in arduous labor, working gladly, not begrudging, seek to serve, and thus be faithful to the high ideals and purpose of the Order of the Arrow.

• All your strength will be required when you face the isolation that a leader often faces. So tonight beneath the heavens sleep alone upon your groundsheet.

The Ordeal has a different meaning to each candidate who completes it. The physical tests are deeply significant. It is a time of deep searching and high resolve; a unique opportunity to experience all the richness and warmth of brotherhood. The candidate needs this experience not only for his own benefit, but also because his Obligation will require unusual devotion to the work of bringing this spirit to his own Scout troop.

The "induction sequence" is at the heart of the Order. The purpose of the induction is to encourage and inspire Arrowmen in the ideals of the Order and Scouting. It is by this method that we also pass along our traditions.

Your induction began with your election by your fellow Scouts. They selected you for your dedication to the ideals of Scouting. They look to you for leadership.

The term "induction sequence" is used in recognition of the fact that events in our induction must necessarily occur in a particular order, not at random. Following your election, you were called out. Then came your Ordeal, which began with the pre-Ordeal ceremony before an unlit fire, and ended with the Ordeal ceremony before a blazing campfire where you accepted the Obligation and received your Ordeal sash.

The next step in your induction is yours to carry out. Think about what you learned at your Ordeal and start applying it to your daily life. When you have made the principles of the Order part of your life, you are ready to complete your induction by "sealing your membership" in the Order of the Arrow through Brotherhood membership.

The purpose of Scouting is to build character, citizenship, and fitness. Camping is one of the most important ways these attributes are learned in the Scouting program. The Order of the Arrow arose in a camping situation, and has kept camping promotion as a major emphasis in order to further the aims of Scouting.

The native American cultures foster a love of the outdoors and nature. They use ceremonies to bind themselves together; to remind themselves of their obligations to themselves and each other. They set aside times for meditation, silence, isolation, fasting, and special duties to the tribe. The Order of the Arrow helps preserve this cultural perspective in camping promotion and induction. While we often celebrate our interest in native American culture with authentic dances and crafts, you do not need Indian attire, or an interest or ability in Indian lore or crafts to be a good Arrowman. Indian lore unto itself is colorful and interesting, but it is the inner strengths and fortitude of native Americans that we seek to place emphasis on. To this end, the Order of the Arrow does more than place an emphasis on camping; it encourages the sort of Scout activity that fosters character development, citizenship training, and physical fitness.

The Ordeal is an adventure of the spirit; a time of deep searching and high resolve; a unique opportunity to experience all of the richness and warmth of brotherhood.

**Order of the Arrow Official Song**
Words by E. Urner Goodman

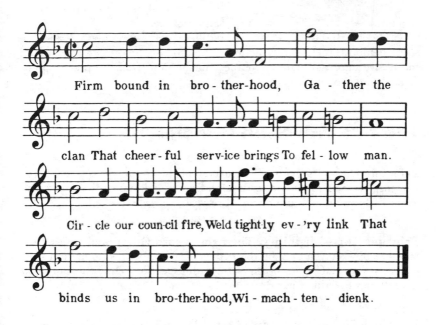

Firm bound in bro-ther-hood, Ga - ther the clan That cheer-ful serv-ice brings To fel - low man. Cir - cle our coun-cil fire, Weld tight-ly ev - 'ry link That binds us in bro-ther-hood, Wi - mach - ten - dienk.

Obtain a copy of *Ceremony for the Ordeal,* No. 5005, to learn more about the significance of the physical tests and each part of the Ordeal. This publication is a resource of information on a variety of topics, including the ceremony and ceremonial grounds setup, the Legend in prose, and a pronunciation guide. The entire ceremony is also included.

The Ten Induction Principles outline the basic philosophy and spirit behind the Ordeal induction. These points help to ensure the impressive nature of our ceremonies and remind us of the process and procedure to follow.

# The Ten Induction Principles

**Principle One—Purpose:** The purpose of the induction is to encourage and inspire each candidate to develop firm individual dedication to the ideals of brotherhood and cheerful service.

**Principle Two—Eligibility:** The right to earn Ordeal and Brotherhood membership is given only by the Scouts of a candidate's home unit during an authorized Order of the Arrow unit election. Only the candidate himself can overrule their decision.

**Principle Three—Candidate's Compliance:** The candidate has the continuous choice of meeting the tests of the Ordeal to the best of his ability or of withdrawing.

**Principle Four—Members' Compliance:** All members participating in the induction must respect and comply with the tests of the Ordeal, to the extent allowed by their responsibilities.

**Principle Five—Discretion:** In cases where strict application of the tests and requirements of the induction is not possible, the lodge may

choose an alternative that will best preserve the spirit of the induction and the quality of the candidate's experience.

**Principle Six—Importance of the Individual:** All actions and procedures must recognize the worth, dignity, and separate identity of the individual and his present or potential ability to govern himself.

**Principle Seven—Generosity:** The attitude of members toward the candidate must be one of acceptance, respect, understanding, sincerity, friendly encouragement, support, and trust.

**Principle Eight—Focus:** Everything in the lodge-created environment must direct the candidate to the central meaning of the induction, and not distract him from it.

**Principle Nine—Symbolic Progression:** No symbol or symbolic procedure should be mentioned or used unless and until it is called for in the authorized ceremonies.

**Principle Ten—Active Membership:** Lodge policy must recognize that if a member understands the obligation of the Order and is striving to fulfill it as an active member, his dedication in itself accomplishes the major service of the lodge.

# History

The Order of the Arrow was founded to serve a useful purpose: Causing the Scout Promise and Law to spring into action in all parts of the nation. To this day, we are dedicated to this high purpose.

The Order is a thing of the individual rather than a thing of the masses. The ideals of brotherhood, cheerfulness, and service spring to life in each of us. What each Arrowman does counts toward the success we have as an organization.

The Order is a thing of the outdoors. It was born in an island wilderness. It needs and is nurtured by the sun and the rain, the mountains and the plains, the woods, the waters, and the starlit sky.

From life in the wilds comes a precious ingredient that our country, and any country, needs to survive—self-reliance, making us strong in times of stress. One of the Order's greatest achievements is, and will continue to be, the strengthening of the Scouting movement as an outdoor experience.

Dr. E. Urner Goodman, founder of the Order of the Arrow, once said:

*The Order is a thing of the spirit rather than of mechanics. Organization, operational procedures, and all that go with them are necessary in any large and growing movement, but they are not what counts in the end. The things of the spirit are what count:*

**Brotherhood**—in a day when there is too much hatred at home and abroad

**Cheerfulness**—in a day when the pessimists have the floor and cynics are popular

**Service**—in a day when millions are interested in getting or grasping, rather than giving

While the Order's role includes service to Scouting on a national, regional, sectional, and local level, it is our own council that needs us most. The Order is not an end unto itself, but is for a higher purpose.

The Order of the Arrow was founded during the summer of 1915 at Treasure Island, the Philadelphia Council Scout camp. Treasure Island was part of the original land grant given to William Penn by King Charles II of England. The camp was located on a 50-acre wooded

**Dr. E. Urner Goodman,**
founder of the
Order of the Arrow

island located in the Delaware River between New Jersey and Pennsylvania, 30 miles upriver from Trenton and 3 miles from Point Pleasant. Historical records show that it was an early camping ground of the Lenni Lanape or Delaware Indians.

In May 1915, a young man named E. Urner Goodman was selected to serve as camp director of Treasure Island for the summer. Another young man, Carroll A. Edson, was appointed assistant director in charge of the commissary. Both men were 24 years old.

Goodman had been a Scoutmaster in Philadelphia and had considerable experience in Scouting and camping. Edson was a graduate of Dartmouth College and had also been in Scouting for several years. After their appointments were announced, they spent many hours together making plans for their summer camping season, and both did considerable reading and research to better prepare themselves for their new responsibilities.

Among the books Goodman read, several were about camping. One of these that impressed him the most, a book dealing with summer camp operation, contained a description of a camp society that had been organized at a camp to perpetuate its traditions and ideals from season to season. Goodman and Edson agreed that they wanted to establish a similar society at their camp. They wanted some definite form of recognition for those Scouts in their camp who best exemplified the spirit of the Scout Oath and Law in their daily lives. Since the Delaware Valley was rich in Indian tradition, and the island had been used in early times as an Indian camping ground, it seemed only natural to base this society, this brotherhood of honor campers, on the legend and traditions of the Delaware Indians.

Shortly after it had been announced that he was selected to serve as assistant camp director, Carroll Edson went home for a weekend visit. During that visit, he attended a meeting where Ernest Thompson Seton, Chief Scout of the Boy Scouts of America, was speaking. Seton described how, when organizing an earlier youth movement called the Woodcraft Indians, he had much success by utilizing Indian ceremonies at camp. This crystallized Goodman and Edson's idea of using the lore and legends of the Delaware Indians in their new brotherhood.

As a result, they prepared a simple yet effective ceremony that, in turn, led to the organization of what was later to become known as the Order of the Arrow. It was agreed from the beginning that the procedures and programs of the organization were to be based on the ideals of democracy. In their initial decisions, Goodman and Edson reflected those ideals by planning to elect members into the first lodge from the troops encamped at Treasure Island. Thus, from the beginning, a unique custom was established in that members were elected by non-members. There has been no change in this since that time. The original name, Wimachtendienk, Wingolauchsik, Witahemui, was suggested by Horace W. Ralston, a Philadelphia Scouter. Ralston and Horace P. Kern had done most of the research on the Delaware Indians.

Soon after camp opened, Goodman explored the island in order to find the most appropriate setting for the ceremonial ground. He selected a site in the south woods of the island, far removed from the ordinary activities of camp, and Edson agreed that it would be an ideal

**Carroll A. Edson**

spot. It was considerably off the beaten path, and because of its location was an excellent site.

The site chosen was a natural amphitheater formed by a ravine in dense woods. There was a clearing there with sloping ground on one side, which lent itself well to spectator seating. The site was cleared of brush and a path cut through thick underbrush from the camp to the site.

Friday, July 16, 1915, dawned bright and clear on Treasure Island. In addition to the heavy heat that often hangs over the valley of the Delaware, there was something else in the air. It was an almost indescribable feeling of expectancy and mystery. By sundown the air was charged with a tense excitement. Those who were present always remembered the first induction into what is now known as the Order of the Arrow.

As darkness fell, the campers were lined up in single file by Harry Yoder, who acted as guide and guardian of the trail. In total silence the campers followed the guide by a roundabout route through the woods to the site of the council fire. The path led down a small ravine across which lay an old fallen tree. The boys were unaware that they were approaching the council fire until suddenly it was revealed. It was built in a triangular shape. Behind it, in long black robes, stood the cofounders of the Order of the Arrow—E. Urner Goodman, Chief of the Fire, and Carroll A. Edson, Vice-chief of the Fire. The Chief of the Fire wore on his robe a turtle superimposed upon a triangle, denoting leadership, and the Vice-chief of the Fire, then called Sachem, wore a turtle without the triangle. (The turtle is the totem of the Unami Lodge.)

The original ceremony was quite different from that which developed later. There were three lessons taught that night:

1. The candidate attempted to encircle a large tree, individually, with outstretched arms. Having failed, he then was joined by several of the brothers who together had no difficulty encircling the large tree, thus teaching lesson No. 1, Brotherhood.

2. The candidate was directed to endeavor to scale a steep bank at the edge of the council ring. Failing in this, he again was assisted by the brothers, with whose help he was able to climb the elevation, thus teaching Service.

3. The candidate then was given a bundle of twigs and told to place some on the council fire, where the twigs caught fire and blazed brightly, thus showing Cheerfulness.

In the first year, 25 members were inducted into the Brotherhood. Many of the members wore a black sash with a white arrow on it. The black sash was used because it offered an excellent contrast to the white arrow. In the original plan there were two degrees; the first was much like a combination of the Ordeal and Brotherhood memberships, and the second an early version of the Vigil Honor.

To perpetuate the brotherhood, a membership meeting was held on November 23, 1915. George W. Chapman, the first lodge chief of Unami Lodge, served as chairman of the organization committee. This meeting marked the first formal founding of the Order of the Arrow. Goodman and Edson served as advisers to the committee.

By 1917, news of the organization, Wimachtendienk, Wingolauchsik, Witahemui, spread to other Scout camps and inquiries began. Goodman spoke to many interested Scouts and Scouters, and as a result, lodges were established in New Jersey, Maryland, New York, and Illinois.

From 1915 until 1921 the Order grew slowly. World War I kept Scouts and leaders busy with many other problems and projects. In 1921 steps were taken to establish the Order on a national basis. The early years had produced sufficient experience to form a foundation on sound basic policies.

The first national convention was held on October 7, 1921, in Philadelphia, at which a national lodge was formed, composed of four delegates from each of the local lodges. This group adopted a constitution and a statement of policies. Committees were appointed to develop plans for making the Order effective as a national honor campers' brotherhood.

Following the convention there was a steady growth in lodges and membership. At the suggestion of the national lodge meeting at Reading, Pa., the Order of the Arrow became an official program experiment of the Boy Scouts of America in 1922.

For several years conventions of the national lodge were held annually. After 1927, they were held at 2-year intervals. During the Philadelphia convention of 1929, it was suggested that the Order become an official part of the Boy Scouts of America and a component part of its program. At the session of the national lodge in 1933, held at the Owasippe Camps of the Chicago Council, this proposal was made and ratified by the delegates.

On June 2, 1934, at the National Council Annual Meeting in Buffalo, N.Y., the Order of the Arrow program was approved by the National Council.

In May 1948, the Executive Board, upon recommendation of its Committee on Camping, officially integrated the Order of the Arrow into the Scouting movement. The Order's national lodge was dissolved and supervision shifted to the Boy Scouts of America.

The executive committee of the national lodge became the national Committee on Order of the Arrow, a subcommittee of the national Committee on Camping and Engineering, and a staff member was employed as national executive secretary. In the 1974 reorganization of the Boy Scouts of America, the national Order of the Arrow committee became a subcommittee of the national Boy Scout Committee.

The growth of the Order of the Arrow through the years has never been based on an aggressive promotional plan. It came about because councils believed in the ideals expressed by the Order and voluntarily requested that lodges be formed. The soundness of providing a single workable honor campers' brotherhood, rather than many, is evident. More than 1 million Boy Scouts, Explorers, and Scouters have been inducted into the Order during the past 70 years. There are now more than 160,000 active members.

# Ties of Brotherhood

To become a member of the Order of the Arrow, you had to be selected by vote of the Scouts or Explorers in your unit. Since most of those who selected you for this honor are not members of this lodge, it is easy to see that the membership is controlled by young men in units and not by those who are already Arrow members.

Always remember that you were honored by your peers, who elected you to the Order because of your camping ability and Scouting spirit.

They set you apart as one from whom they expect much. They expect you to give leadership in camping and cheerful service.

You must resolve, therefore, not to let them down!

## The Ordeal

After election, a Boy Scout, Varsity Scout, Explorer, or Scouter is considered a candidate until he has completed the Ordeal of the Order.

**Purpose of the Ordeal.** It is the purpose of the Ordeal to have the candidate reflect on his own Scout life and character and come to a deeper understanding of the Scout Oath or Promise and the principles of the Order. This purpose is realized through a fourfold Ordeal that includes sleeping alone, silence, work, and a limited amount of food.

The candidate spends a night alone as proof of his courage and self-reliance. It also gives him a chance to think over clearly the events taking place.

The candidate keeps complete silence. This gives him the opportunity to pay stricter attention to his unspoken thoughts, searching out his past deficiencies and resolving on a life of fuller service in the future.

The candidate spends the daylight hours of his Ordeal in meaningful labor. This proves his willingness to serve his fellowman cheerfully.

The candidate also eats sparingly, thus proving his ability to subordinate the appetites of the body to the high purposes of the spirit.

Taken together, the four elements of the Ordeal are a meaningful and inspiring experience for the candidate. They provide a total participation of the mind and spirit. The Ordeal is not soon forgotten by the new member.

**Ordeal membership.** The steps required to complete the Ordeal membership are defined clearly. Once a person has been elected to the Order of the Arrow by his unit members, he is formally recognized as a candidate. This is done at a calling-out ceremony, usually conducted by the ceremonies team in an outdoor setting. The candidate then takes part in a brief pre-Ordeal ceremony, and then an actual Ordeal (series of tests) to prove his sincere dedication to the principles of the Order of the Arrow. Finally, if he qualifies, he is accepted as a member in a colorful ceremony.

**Calling out.** Many lodges have developed their own calling-out ceremonies, which might be done at camp during the evening assembly in the dining hall, or at some other activity and place. Calling-out ceremonies also have been developed for camporees and district or council events. Suggestions are available in the *Administration Guide for the Ordeal*.

At times the pre-Ordeal and Ordeal ceremonies are held during the evening and night of the day following the calling out. If so, the candidates are instructed in advance by an Ordeal master. If some time is to elapse before the ceremonies, the following information should be sent by mail to each candidate:

1. Notice that he has been selected by his fellow campers. This should be done regardless of whether he was told at the time of the election.

2. Specific date, place, and time that he should report for the Ordeal.

3. Instructions that the candidate come fully prepared with blankets or sleeping bag and a ground cloth for an overnight campout alone in the open, and a change of clothing suitable for a day's labor.

4. Notice of all costs that the candidate will be expected to pay, including sash, manual, food, etc.

**Ordeal master's job.** The Ordeal master, a young man younger than 21, is appointed by the lodge chief with the advice of the lodge adviser. He will have charge of the candidates during the pre-Ordeal and Ordeal.

He should be a mature member with good judgment and have full authority to make changes in the Ordeal procedure to meet with varying situations, such as severe weather conditions or the candidate's physical condition. A candidate's health should not be endangered by the conditions under which the Ordeal is conducted.

The Ordeal master must conduct the Ordeal on a high standard with **no hazing.** Extreme care should be taken that each candidate fully understands the symbolism of the pre-Ordeal ceremony and the reason for all Ordeal tests. He makes sure that each candidate knows why he spent a night alone, why he was required to spend a day in silence, and why he spent the day working.

The entire pre-Ordeal and Ordeal should be conducted in a remote part of camp; if possible in an area rarely used by anyone. No effort should be made to tease or tempt a candidate to break his pledge of silence or to eat more food than officially authorized by the Ordeal master.

The Scout executive, camp director, and Ordeal master and his assistants have the right to suspend the "no talking" rule should an emergency arise.

**Ordeal projects.** Meaningful projects should be a concern of the Ordeal master and his assistants. The candidates should feel that they are making a positive contribution to the camp. Advance planning is a must.

Candidates should be matched with projects they are capable of handling. Be sure that the necessary equipment and supplies are on hand so that no time is lost.

Adult candidates should be given adult-type projects and an adult should be assigned as the Ordeal master for all adult candidates.

**Spirit of the Arrow.** The *Spirit of the Arrow* pamphlets are a method of preparing Ordeal candidates for membership in the Order of the Arrow.

These pamphlets are a handy aid for Ordeal candidates, enabling them to discover the meaning of their experiences while they are actually taking part in the silent portion of the Ordeal. Lodges using the Spirit of the Arrow material report that candidates who use individual booklets do so willingly with fine results.

The *Spirit of the Arrow* pamphlets are a self-training device that helps the candidate understand the deepest and most inspirational meanings of the Ordeal. The pamphlets are given to the candidates at specified times during the Ordeal. Copies may be obtained through your council service center.

**The Ordeal and the induction.** Just as the induction is at the heart of the Order, the Ordeal is at the heart of the induction. You first experienced the Order in the Ordeal. You lived our principles and traditions. At the same time, existing members recharged themselves. Now, your study and application of the Ordeal's lessons guide you. Its tests model our continuous conduct as Arrowmen. Thus, the Ordeal was not only your conduit into the Order, it will remain a channel for your Order of the Arrow experiences.

Begin now by recalling your own Ordeal. Then read this section to compare your experience with that of thousands of Arrowmen before you. Finally, decide how to use your new understanding.


**Evening of the pre-Ordeal.** After check-in and probably a long wait, you were taken to a strange clearing in the woods. At the center of a circle was an unlit fire. Light came from 15 blazes forming the circle and representing the Scout Oath and Law.

Four figures in ceremonial attire stood around the fire lay. Kichkinet, in the East, is your guide in the ceremonies. He symbolizes helpfulness and friendliness. Nutiket, in the South, is the guard of the circle. He upholds the tradition of cheerfulness. Meteu, in the West, is the medicine man and represents Brotherhood. He reminds us to love one another. Allowat Sakima, in the North, is the mighty chief, and exemplifies Service.

Each one spoke to you. Nutiket told of the scant food test. He flexed a bow as a token of liveliness and flexibility under stress, the principle of Cheerfulness. He then gave the bow to Allowat Sakima. Meteu pledged you to silence and displayed a bowstring as a token of the ties of Brotherhood. He also passed his token to Allowat Sakima.

Allowat Sakima spoke of the day of work and strung the bow uniting Brotherhood and Cheerfulness. He was wearing a quiver of arrows representing the burden of service he carries as chief. He drew one arrow from the quiver as a token that your election separated you from your fellow Scouts for something higher. He asked you to test the bow to show your willingness to try your dedication to Scout ideals. Lastly, Kichkinet shot the arrow upward, symbolizing the pathway you follow if your dedication is unwavering. He told of your need to spend the night alone. Saying, "Let us try to find the Arrow!" he led you away from the circle.

Your guide set you out alone for the night. In the future you will separate yourself. As a leader, you will occasionally make unpopular decisions. You may need to "leave the crowd and its opinions." This will be hard and unpleasant, and others may treat you roughly. Again, you can show the courage that you showed on your night alone. You can rescue yourself from complete isolation with the self-reliance you used when your guide set you apart.

**Day of the Ordeal.** You pledged yourself to silence for the Ordeal. Did you notice how the silence bound you to the other candidates, and made you more aware of their needs? The Ordeal illustrates the value of getting away from the noisy confusion of life. Time in thoughtful silence helps you with difficult decisions. When you have an important choice, stop and listen. We all make mistakes. But most errors occur when we rush off without hearing our small, inner voice.

Your day of work showed your willingness to serve, even when service involves hardship and toil, or seems dumb and boring. In the Ordeal you had help and cooperation from others, but in Scouting and daily life, you will often serve without them. Prepare to give more difficult service, like befriending a Scout others are teasing.

The scant food test illustrates self-denial. You will abandon personal comfort and momentary desires to achieve goals. On your quest do not merely help others, but do so willingly and cheerfully. When uncomfortable or frustrated, when giving up a personal desire, this test challenges again.

Just as you did all four tests; separation, silence, arduous labor, and scant food; together during the Ordeal, you will find them useful together in daily life. Consider silence and separation. You need time alone every day. Some Arrowmen use a few minutes to review their Good Turns and misdeeds each day, guided by their sense of right and wrong. Then they set goals and make plans. Thinking alone without the noisy intrusions of the outside world joins the tests of silence and isolation. You should maintain a regular habit of taking stock of yourself alone with your God.

**Evening of the Ordeal.** As on the previous evening, you were taken to a special place. This time, however, you placed a hand on the shoulder of the Scout in front of you. This was a token of your intention to continue in service to your troop. Then you were bound by a rope representing brotherhood. Finally, you advanced toward the fire of cheerfulness. With these three acts you prepared symbolically to receive the Obligation of the Order.

After you took upon yourself your solemn Obligation, Meteu gave you the legend of how the Order was founded. He spoke of the peaceful Lenni Lenape (the Delaware Indians), their chief, Chingachgook, and the chief's son, Uncas. When war threatened, Chingachgook sought volunteers to alert other villages, but few saw danger. Most were apathetic, only wanting to enjoy their life at home. However, Uncas had a higher vision of life. He cheerfully offered his help despite the negative attitudes around him. He cared enough for others that he was willing to face hardship and life-threatening danger, alone if necessary.

Uncas, Chingachgook, and others with like motives gave self-sacrificing service, and the fierce marauders were compelled to retire to their own country. When peace returned, to maintain and spread the shared vision of cheerful service, Chingachgook bound Uncas and those who joined him together as brothers. The Lenni Lenape named this brotherhood Wimachtendienk, Wingolauchsik, Witahemui. Today, you carry on its traditions in the Order of the Arrow.

Allowat Sakima then described the Arrow as being "straight, its point keen. Aimed high, its course is undeviating, its direction onward and upward." He whispered a single word in your ear, our Admonition, which is the key to the Order. He also gave you the handclasp of the Order with its two interlocked fingers representing the bonds of Brotherhood. Finally, you received your Ordeal sash.

Ordeal sash

**Keeping the legend of the Order alive.** Do you hope to serve your community? Can you make a contribution such as that made by Uncas and Chingachgook? "Neighboring tribes and distant enemies" may not seem to threaten your "peaceful way of life." Yet the challenges are there for far-sighted leaders to find and attack. Will you play the role of Chingachgook who first saw the problem and sounded the alarm? Or of Uncas who cheerfully offered his services when others would not? Or will you hide in the nameless crowd?

Dedicated people continue to make admirable contributions to humanity through lifetimes of cheerful, self-sacrificing service. Mohandas Gandhi led the nonviolent movement for freedom of the Indian subcontinent. Albert Schweitzer gave medical service in Africa. Dietrich Bonhoffer preached and acted against Hitler within Nazi Germany. Martin Luther King, Jr., lead the American civil rights movement. Each led a life worthy of your study. Each was controversial in his day. Each, in his own way, espoused the principles of the Order and lived the tests of the Ordeal. Who of your heros could you add to this group? For each of the prominent people who can be named as having led a worthy life of service to others, tens of thousands, indeed millions, of others have likewise made a difference. You can be one of these. How will future generations judge your contribution?

**Mystery and the Ordeal.** As a member of the Order, you have undergone tests and ceremonies which challenged you and helped you to think about your life. The mystery in which we cloak these steps is part of the induction. Scouts receive less benefit if they know about the induction in advance. Most every candidate feels anxiety about the unknown as he approaches his Ordeal. Knowledge lowers expectancy, dulling the edge of experience. In other words, you hurt a Scout when you tell him about the Ordeal. He is better off knowing nothing until he receives the challenges from the age-old figures in the pre-Ordeal ceremony.

Be vague when answering questions from a fellow Scout about the Ordeal. Do not even confirm or deny what he thinks he knows. Smiling pleasantly (as you remember the great time you had!) and changing the subject is best. Leaving a sense of mystery adds to the Order of the Arrow for everyone. You have earned the right to learn about the Order, including the Ordeal; those who have not been elected have not. Exposing our special things is unfair to everyone.

Stretching the truth or just plain lying about the Order or the Ordeal is not Scoutlike. If you cause a candidate to worry about something that is not part of the Ordeal, you have distracted him from his purpose. And that hurts everyone!

On the other hand, the Order of the Arrow recognizes the right of interested adults to learn about our purpose and methods. Feel free to discuss your experiences with your parents.

**Attending the Ordeal as a member.** Every Ordeal requires detailed planning, extensive training, and careful preparation. Presenting a good one is difficult and complex. It must go so smoothly that the candidates are not aware of the complex administrative problems.

Taking the part of Allowat Sakima, Meteu, Nutiket, or Kichkinet is a rewarding job. But it requires commitment. Memorization is easy only if you begin months ahead. Team members study the meanings of the lines, practice delivery and movements, and become emotionally involved in conveying the message to the candidates.

Serving as an Elangomat, "friend" in the language of the Lenni Lenape, is also rewarding and challenging. As an Elangomat, you go through the tests of the Ordeal along with the candidates. Your example is a better teacher of Brotherhood, Cheerfulness, and Service than any spoken words. By learning more about the Order and yourself, you also rededicate yourself to the Order. Dedication to the ideals of the Order is the hallmark of a good Elangomat.

Each Elangomat generally leads a patrol-size group of candidates, often called a "clan." When the lodge uses them, each clan is independent from the others. Since an Elangomat shares the test of silence and cannot easily ask questions, the lodge trains him in advance. During the Ordeal the lodge provides him close support to meet any needs.

A successful Ordeal also has many behind-the-scenes accomplishments. Brothers cook food, prepare sashes and supplies, complete records, issue membership cards, build and extinguish fires, and so on. Many helpful members make a complete Ordeal.

Every member must be an Elangomat at times. We have grown in understanding since our Ordeals. We recognize the significance of the tests more than at first. Thus, when near candidates, we share the tests wholeheartedly. A spirit of seriousness and commitment, seen by the candidates in each member, shows them that the tests are not a joke or harassment but an important pointer to a valuable way of life.

**Compliance with the Ordeal.** From the time of election through the pre-Ordeal and Ordeal, including the Ordeal ceremony, all candidates should be able to qualify for all the tests of the Ordeal. Rarely is there a violation of the spirit of the Ordeal so flagrant as to make a candidate unworthy. When this happens the candidate usually withdraws without being asked, because he realizes his own shortcomings.

The Ordeal master should report all violations to the lodge adviser or camp director, who may wish to discuss the matter privately with the candidate involved. It must be remembered that the lodge members cannot vote to accept or reject a candidate properly elected by his fellow campers.

**Why ceremonies?** The ceremonies of the Order of the Arrow were developed to help members learn and feel its high purpose. They are not meant to imitate the induction procedures of adult fraternal groups. The following policy on safeguarding all ceremonial concepts and material should be exercised. Youth and adults elected into this program have earned the exclusive privilege of learning these concepts aimed at developing leadership abilities through a safeguarded ceremonial induction. Passwords, signs and countersigns, and secluded sites all are a part of the ceremonies, and nonmembers should respect the safeguarding of these procedures. The Order's ceremonies are not public nor are they in any way meant to be a social affair. You always should be able to answer yes to Allowat Sakima's question, "Are you Brothers satisfied that all present are members?"

Although the contents of the ceremonies are private, they were written to avoid offending any religious belief and have received the approval of religious leaders. The ceremonies are true to Scout tradition and within the spirit of the Scout Oath and Law.

We recognize and respect the right of any parent, Scout leader, or religious leader to be concerned about the content of the ceremonies. Lodge advisers will willingly discuss the content of the ceremony and any other concerns brought to their attention. If after the discussion, a request to attend an Order of the Arrow ceremony is received from any sincerely interested adult, permission will be granted with the understanding that the visitor must not interfere with the ceremony.

**Become active.** Your lodge (and/or chapter) needs your help for it to be successful. You can acknowledge the honor bestowed upon you by your fellow Scouts by becoming an active Arrowman, providing leadership to your unit or Scouting function. Become involved in your lodge by attending meetings and serving on one or more of its committees.

The Order of the Arrow program allows opportunities for members younger than 21 to serve in leadership positions and those 21 and older to lend their knowledge and experience to the youth as advisers.

Committees of all interest areas have been specifically designed to utilize the varied skills and interests of new members. You will meet and make new friends as well as find the experience rewarding.

Whether your goal is to serve others, to lead, to learn more about leadership, or to learn more about yourself, you will find it in the Order.

# You, Your Lodge, and Scouting

**You and your unit.** An Arrowman's primary responsibility is to his troop, team or post. It was your fellow Scouts or Explorers who elected you to membership in the Order and it is to them that you should devote most of your service.

Your fellow Scouts elected you to membership because of your Scout spirit and camping ability. They set you apart as one from whom they expect a great deal. Your experience with the Ordeal should enable you now to give the leadership they want and expect from you. For this reason, your first duty as an Arrowman is to continue to expand your service to your unit. The success of the Order in your unit depends mainly on what you do individually. Your example of cheerful service in camp and at unit meetings is the spark that brings the spirit alive!

Dr. E. Urner Goodman, founder of the Order, once said: "Let it be remembered that the Order of the Arrow was created to help the unit—to help it present its membership a better idea of the inner qualities of the good Scout camper.

"Qualities of character, like cheerfulness and service, are hard for a boy or a man to understand in the abstract. They come easier when seen in human life.

"The Order was started to help glorify these qualities of the good Scout camper in the unit, so that they might be appreciated there, not only during the brief term in summer camp but all of the days and the weeks of the year.

"Let us realize the significance of the Order in the unit—for the unit is our best hope in Scouting . . ."

What are your responsibilities to your unit? You should make sure that your unit maintains an active camping program and that as many members of the unit as possible are involved. Be sure your lodge or chapter camp promotion team visits your unit at least once a year and that you have an annual Order of the Arrow election for membership. Your unit should help the lodge give service to as many community service projects as possible. It is also important that you keep your unit members informed on current happenings of the lodge and local council.

You were a leader in your troop before the Scouts elected you to the Order. Your membership does not change your position in your troop, but the Order does affect your relationship to it. As an Arrowman, you have new responsibilities to your troop and a different point of view.

## Being a Leader

**Setting the example.** Example setting is central to the methods of the Order. The members of your troop elected you because they look up to you. Your job is to live up to their high expectations—to serve them by being the best example of the Scout Oath and Law in action that you possibly can.

The Scout Oath and Law are the center of Scouting. But they are mere words for new Scouts until they see these ideals in the actions of troop leaders. This means YOU! How much will "trustworthy" mean if they see you cheat to give your patrol more points? How much will "helpful" mean if you don't work with them on advancement? Or "cheerful" if you get angry when the weather turns bad on a campout or you get stuck with an extra turn of cleaning the dishes?

None of us is perfect. The Order helps us to remind each other that younger Scouts imitate us. We each strive to listen to our personal sense of right and wrong so that others will see a good Scout in action. By electing you to the Order, they entrusted you with this important task. Don't let them down.

**Leadership in your troop.** As your interest in the welfare of your troop and in its members grows, you will take on more difficult leadership roles. You may move up to higher positions in the troop or accept increasingly harder jobs. As an Arrowman, do not just take on more, but look for unwanted, yet needed, tasks. Seek ways to offer friendship and brotherhood as you lead. Maintain a cheerful outlook no matter how difficult the situation.

You need special skills as you endeavor to lead your troop in an ethical manner. Giving friendship, running meetings fairly, helping a friend solve problems, sharing skills with others, and building a camping troop, all help you as you lead your troop and as you complete your personal quest.

**Giving friendship.** All you will do as an Arrowman starts with giving friendship. In turn, your friendship arises from your basic values. Your religious beliefs and moral convictions influence all you think and say and do. Thus, your friendship should be morally sound, predictably strong, and respectful of others. All this makes your gift of friendship invaluable. It will often return to you greatly increased, but don't limit or stunt friendship by giving it only in expectation of return.

Be so constant in your friendship that others can predict your actions in any given situation. When you smile every day at your teachers, they can expect a cheerful outlook during final exams. When you make a new Scout comfortable at his first troop meetings, he can expect to feel at home on his first campout. When you react calmly to small problems, your friends ask you for help in an emergency.

Respect the rights and beliefs of others. Treasure the differences. Learn to enjoy the company of those who are unlike you. Try to generate light rather than heat when discussing politics, religion, or other value-laden subjects. If a friend's behavior bothers you, tell him, but never question the sincerity of his motives.

Do not go along when others suggest anything that you consider wrong. Attempt, if you wish, to persuade them that their actions will be wrong. But if necessary, distance yourself from them until another day.

As you practice giving friendship, you master the mechanics that are part of it. Many of them are points of the Scout Law. Smile whenever you can. Learn the name of each person you meet and use it often when talking with him. (Learning names is work, but it shows your sincerity.) Actively listen to others and encourage them to talk about themselves and their interests. Do not turn private conversations into gossip. Take your burden and then some when there is work to be done. Promptly thank others for any kindness. Encourage bystanders to participate. Each of these are valuable habits of giving friendship, and each of the following sections has more.

Cultivate the habits of giving friendship. Right now can you pick your strongest habit of friendship? pick your weakest habit of friendship?

At the end of each day, review these two habits. Recall the events of the day and ask yourself: When was I especially good at each habit? When was I especially bad? What was different about me that made me act properly one time and poorly the other? How will I try to do better tomorrow? When you have improved both habits, choose two more and improve them the same way.

Through conscious daily effort you can make a good habit part of yourself or break a bad habit. As long as your friendship rises from deeply held convictions, it shows.


**How to run a meeting fairly.** The great deliberative bodies of the world, especially the British Parliament and the United States Congress, have developed procedures to ensure fairness to all. Some of these date back hundreds of years—those in the United States to the days of Thomas Jefferson.

If you are leading a small group, such as a patrol, you have a greater challenge than just chairing the meeting fairly. Experienced leaders know that all members of a small group must agree if it is to function effectively. Therefore, they work toward unanimous decisions. This not only strengthens the group and its ability to function, but also generates many ideas.

Here are fundamental procedures for running any meeting impartially and smoothly.

- Have an agenda worked out in advance. Include each subject that you know any member wants to discuss. Rank the subjects with the most important first, and stick to this order. Don't allow discussion on other subjects until the end, when the agenda should have time listed for "other new business."

- Keep to one subject at a time. If the meeting is large or formal, or discussion is disorderly, require that a motion be made and seconded before allowing any discussion, and limit speakers to the motion.

- Keep each motion simple. The purpose is to focus discussion and to have specific words on which to vote. You may help by suggesting the motion. You say, "The chair will entertain a motion to camp every month this year (or whatever). Will anyone make this motion?"

- Give everyone a chance to speak. Encourage everyone to understand all points of view. Avoid giving your personal opinions unless it is a small, informal meeting. A chairman tries to be impartial.

- After everyone has said everything they wish, put the motion to a vote. Restate the motion, then ask for "ayes," then "nays" using a show of hands in a large meeting. (If anyone requests a secret ballot, have one.) State the results.

- The members can only force an end to discussion by a two-thirds vote (at least twice as many voting to end discussion as voting to continue). People often confuse voting to end discussion with voting on the motion itself. Always state what a particular "yes" vote will do. Here, it ends debate and forces a vote on the original motion.

  You do not need a vote to end the discussion. When no one wants to speak, say "Is there any more discussion? (Pause) Seeing none, let's vote on the motion to spend two weeks at camp (or whatever)."

- When debate is unproductive and there are more crucial issues, suggest that the group "table the motion until (a particular time)." This motion requires a simple majority. Remind the group that a "yes" vote stops discussion until the particular time. Reopen the discussion when the time agreed upon arrives.

  When members have strong opinions and are not understanding one another, suggest tabling the motion until the beginning of the next meeting. Encourage another, informal, meeting devoted to understanding points of view.

Remember, your job as chairman is to help the majority make decisions while protecting the rights of the minority. You are most successful when you help the group agree on compromises so that all can win.

At the completion of every meeting, review the meeting and your part in it. What were the goals of those present? What importance did group members place on each agenda item? Was everyone able to express himself on issues he felt strongly about? What did you do to make the meeting run fairly and smoothly? What compromises did you suggest that helped the group reach decisions? Who viewed you as an unfair chairman? Who would be willing to meet again under your leadership? What additional preparation should you do for next time?

**Hints on helping a friend in need.** Knowing that you are a decent, trustworthy person, someone may turn to you for help when he is troubled or has a problem. Be open to help. Give him a chance to speak with you alone. Respect his right to privacy.

Be careful not to seem critical of him; he needs a friend, not a judge. Picture yourself in his situation and try to understand how he feels.

If he has done something wrong, don't moralize. Once he realizes he has made a mistake, he needs to figure out how to set it right. Don't kick him while he is down; help him up.

Whether a person has a problem to solve or just needs to talk, a friend can help most by just listening. Let him do most of the talking. Encourage him to explain himself fully. Often explaining a problem solves it.

Avoid giving advice. A person with a problem must arrive at his own decision, one that is right for him. You may make suggestions to start him thinking clearly and creatively. Encourage him to think of many possible solutions, even wild ones. But don't push or pretend you have the answers. He will probably resist advice, even if correct. He will have more confidence in himself and in his decision if he reaches it himself after considering many alternatives.

Be a mirror, not a judge or a know-it-all.

Suppose a friend *tells* you that he is involved in something that is not Scout-like. Because you do not discuss private conversations with nonparticipants, you are on the spot. First, make sure the facts are clear to both you and your friend. Second, encourage your friend to take corrective action himself. Finally, if others are endangered and your friend does not take corrective action, you must take common-sense action. Go to a parent, Scoutmaster, religious leader, or other adult you trust for more help.

Every time you discuss a problem with a friend think about it afterwards. How did you give solid, supportive friendship? What habits of friendship did you use? What pitfalls mentioned above did you fall into? What alternative solutions did you help him explore? What, if any, commitments did you make?

**Hints on how to teach a skill to a Scout.** Before you attempt to teach a skill to someone else, test yourself. Your mental or written answers will help you teach more successfully. How does the Scout literature describe the skill? What are the safety practices? What are three ways the Scout can apply the skill? Did you follow safety practices? Do you need practice before teaching?

First: Get the Scout to understand how much he does and doesn't know. Get him curious while you discover his skill level. Ask him if he can do the skill, and if he says yes, give him a chance to show you. Adjust your plan to his skill level.

Second: Show him how to do it. Don't just talk. Show him how, slowly. Have him watch from a different angle as you show him again. Point out safety rules as you go.

Third: Let him do it. Help only as needed. But watch carefully.

Fourth: Let him test himself—have him do it without help. Make it a game!

Finally: When you are all done, evaluate your own performance. What evidence is there that you both had a good time? What part of the skill do you need to polish up on? What did you do that most maintained his attention? What goofs do you want to avoid next time? What could he do when you started? When you finished?

Ask your Scoutmaster or senior patrol leader for as many instructor assignments as possible; one every troop meeting is not too many. Occasionally, ask someone you consider a good instructor to observe from a distance and evaluate your efforts. As you gain confidence ask the Scout for his evaluation of your teaching. The more you think about and work at teaching, the better instructor you will become.

**Troop camping traditions.** Developing and maintaining camping traditions is one of the purposes of the Order. Every good Scout troop has special camping traditions of its own. Traditions help bind the troop together from year to year. They add quality and sparkle to the troop program. Scouts like them, and anticipate having the same fun they had last time.

Here are examples of traditions from around the nation. Each is a source of deep pride for those troops that follow it. You may find some a bit unusual, but use those to stimulate your imagination.

- Go camping every month.

- Attend summer camp each year.

- Go on a survival camping trip every August.

- Never camp twice in the same place within a year.

- Have a long weekend backpacking trip twice a year.

- Always cook by patrol, even at summer camp.

- Never call off a camping trip because of bad weather, except hurricane, tornado, or blizzard.

- Have a special 50-miler each year for those Scouts meeting requirements in attendance or advancement set by the troop.

- Once each year each patrol has its own campout.

- Do a service project for a local hiking trail as part of a camping trip each year.

- Always cook breakfast and supper from scratch.

- Hike every marked trail at summer camp each summer.

- Give each patrol a distinct campsite, slightly apart from the others.

- Always hike into the campsite.

- Work on advancement on every campout, even camporees.

- Hold a snow camping trip each year.

- Always camp in ponchos, never in tents.

- Take a hike on every campout.

- Have patrol competition on each campout.

- Watch sunrise or sunset from a special spot.

- Attend the national jamboree as a troop.

# Promoting Camping

**Camping promotion.** Camping provided the environment for you to learn to work as a member of a group, to discover new places and friends, and to grow by becoming aware of your abilities. Because you learned these lessons, your troop elected you to the Order. In your Ordeal, camping again provided the time and place for growth.

Your task now is to enhance the camping program of your troop so that other Scouts learn, discover, and grow as you did. This may seem difficult, since the goal is vague and the effect of your efforts hard to observe. But, here are some effective ways to improve camping that can make a real difference.

- Encourage camping. As a member of the Order of the Arrow, you are a respected member of your troop. Other Scouts look up to you. Thus you can enhance camping by simply supporting patrol and troop campouts enthusiastically. Your enthusiasm for camping — especially when things aren't going right — can make a tremendous difference in how others feel about it.

- Improve your camping skills. Can you identify most of the trees you see while camping? Can you start a fire with flint and steel? Do you always wash your dishes properly? Do you use topographic maps often enough to use them well? You can learn a lot from the *Boy Scout Handbook* and the *Fieldbook*. To become good at a skill, you may need to do some library research or to find someone (perhaps another Arrowman) who can give you some pointers. This is part of the fun. But above all, practice! You can't be an expert at everything. But you can find one or two skills that aren't well known in your troop and learn all you can about them. Once you know them, use these skills often and enthusiastically.

- Help new Scouts with camping skills and jobs. Camping isn't fun if you don't know how. Show a new Scout how to enjoy his first camp-out — how to make a comfortable bed on the ground, cook a hearty meal, start a fire, and track a bird or animal. You will find that teaching helps you sharpen your own abilities.

There are always tasks that no one enjoys: hauling water, washing dishes, latrine duty. If you are in charge, make sure these tasks are fairly divided. Don't ask a Scout to do more than he is physically able.

Five gallons of water (about 40 pounds) is a lot to carry for a Scout weighing little more. If a task must be done in a certain way, make sure the Scout knows it. Finally, as an Arrowman, you should enthusiastically help new Scouts with these tasks.

- Encourage variety in camping. Look for new places to camp, and suggest a variety of campout themes and activities. Talk to Arrowmen in other troops and read BSA and other camping literature for ideas. If your parents belong to an auto club, ask them to get you the club's camping guide for the area. Encourage your troop to try new, exciting, and different types of camping experiences by making detailed suggestions.

- Promote good camping traditions. Does your troop have any camping traditions? Things that make your troop special? Don't let them be forgotten over the years. Think about the best times you've had while camping with your troop. Make sure the new Scouts have similar experiences. When your troop does something that makes everyone feel proud, suggest creating a new tradition around it.

  On the other hand, do your best to discourage bad traditions. Initiations, teasing, or harassment of new Scouts have no place in a Scout camp. Even the traditional campfire ghost story can make sleeping away from the comforts of home a scary proposition. Small incidents that make Scouts unhappy can sour them on camping and undo all your positive efforts.

- Promote camping personally. Notice which members of the troop go camping and which do not. Without getting pushy, talk to a Scout who isn't camping and try to find out why he chooses not to. Perhaps he has a problem to resolve (like the ghost story mentioned above.) Showing concern often is enough to make a difference.

- Go camping. Don't just talk about it. Go!

## A Summer Camp Promotion Sales Plan

- To be a successful salesman, you must believe in your product. You can't sell summer camp unless you believe in camp yourself. Spend some silent time alone thinking about what you like about camp and the great times you have had.

- Put up an attractive camping poster in your troop meeting room. You might want to feature pictures of your troop at summer camp. Such a poster is a weekly visual reminder of the fun you had at summer camp. When a Scout commits to going, have him sign up. Make sure that your name is at the head of the list. The earlier you start, the better. The first troop meeting in September is none too early if a Scout works to pay his own way.

- Ask each troop member if he is going to camp. Some wouldn't miss it for anything; they're already sold. Recognize their commitment and show them sincere appreciation. Then call on them to encourage others. Some will never go; you're seeking those Scouts who aren't sure. List these "May Bees" as you find them. When you have several you are ready to achieve success.

- Talk to each May Bee privately. Find out what his interests are. Discover why he is hesitant about going. Are his friends going? Will there be others his age going? Is there something he has heard about camp that worries him?

Remember that a Scout goes to camp for a good time. Stories of your good times are the best evidence of fun at camp. Don't try to sell him the whole camp. Find out what he likes, and sell him those parts of camp that appeal to him. When he believes he will have fun, he'll decide to go. Even if he doesn't go, if you do it right, you will have given friendship. And that's worthwhile.

**Scout campfires.** The campfire has been a focal point in Scouting since the days when Robert Baden-Powell invented Scout camping on Brownsea Island. Whether at the patrol campsite or in the dim evening shadows of the Ordeal, the spirit of Scouting is born in the fire and carried on its smoke. Songs, skits, stories, and silly yells tie each Scout to the tradition of cheerfulness. The fire itself directs the pageantry and symbolizes the day's activities, beginning with its lively crackling start, through a period of bright light and merriment, yielding slowly to a glow of embers.

A successful campfire requires planning and organization. A few key activities provide the framework for a memorable evening. Just as no two fires are built of identical wood, no two scripts should be the same. However, they have similar parts whether the group is large or small, old friends or new. After the opening is a lively period of fun and Scout songs as we use our own energy to excite the flames. As the fire burns low we enjoy a slower time of soft-spoken stories, songs, dreams, and memories as we relax in the satisfaction of a completed day.

The closing of the campfire instills the flame of Scouting in each Scout and ends his day with a moment of inspiration and reverence.

The *Boy Scout Handbook* and the *Fieldbook* both discuss fire building and fire safety. The log-cabin or council fire lay is the best for campfires. You can change the fire size to match the group size. The base of the fire is three or four layers of split, well-dried wood. (Mix quick- and slow-burning woods if the program will be lengthy and the woods are available.) A tepee fire is often built on top of the well-packed lower layers. The quick-starting tepee fire establishes an initial mood of cheerfulness, and its coals catch the lower layers.

The campfire is a symbolic meeting place and a source of light. The audience can see the action any place around a small fire. Thus, it is better than a raging inferno. For a campfire for a large group, use two fires with a distance of about 15 feet between them. If you raise the fires on two fireproof platforms, you provide even better lighting. However, the Ordeal ceremony has only a single council fire at the center of the circle.

Some folks think that a proper campfire requires the smell of kerosene. However, for the sake of safety, limit artificial materials in the fire to wax or paper. Dramatic fire lightings are fun, but make sure they are safe and will work. Always have an alternate plan. Have the fire going well as the first Scouts enter the campfire circle. You then can have your opening ceremony well lit and focus on the message of the ceremony rather than the mechanics of getting the fire to go.

The *Patrol Leader Handbook* is an excellent source of ideas for campfire programs. The *Scoutmaster Handbook* has hints on ceremonies and Scoutmaster minutes that you can adapt to the setting. The best source of material is your imagination and that of your fellow Scouts. Television, movies, and the events of the day provide wonderful opportunities for humorous skits and stories. However, if you are in charge, know what each performer will be doing. Check each plan to maintain the highest of Scouting traditions.

Review the *Boy Scout Handbook* and the *Fieldbook* for ideas for inspirational closings. With advance research, you can tell about someone quoted in the *Fieldbook,* or one of the Americans pictured in the *Boy Scout Handbook.*


**You and your lodge.** Members of the Order of the Arrow are organized into groups called "lodges." Each lodge has its own name and distinctive emblem, also called a totem.

Nearly all councils of the Boy Scouts of America have an Order of the Arrow lodge. Each council chooses whether or not to have a lodge. The Boy Scouts of America charters only one lodge per council. The council must recharter its lodge annually.

The council administers the Order of the Arrow within the council as part of its camping program. The Scout executive is the Supreme Chief of the Fire; the final authority within the council for the Order of the Arrow. He appoints the adult leader of the lodge, the lodge adviser, who serves as Deputy Supreme Chief of the Fire. The lodge adviser acts on behalf of the Scout executive in guiding the day-to-day affairs of the lodge. Other advisers are appointed to assist the lodge adviser in carrying out his responsibilities. Due to the burden of his responsibilities, the Scout executive may delegate his duties with the lodge to another professional staff member, naming him lodge staff adviser.

The Order of the Arrow is a program designed for youth. All lodge and chapter officers and committee chairmen *must* be under the age of 21 during their entire term of office, and must have achieved the First Class rank. Adults serve in advisory capacities only. The officers plan and conduct all meetings and events, as well as develop and fund an annual operating budget.

Lodges may choose to divide into chapters. In such cases, often there is one chapter for each district. Each chapter has its own officers and advisers. Like the lodge, all chapter officers and committee chairmen *must* be younger than 21 during their entire term of office, and must have achieved the First Class rank. In this case, the Scout executive appoints a chapter adviser and chapter staff adviser (who often is a district executive).

Each lodge (and chapter) is run by the youth members, under 21 years of age. Only those younger than 21 may hold office or vote on any action. Elected lodge officers include the chief, one or more vice chiefs, a secretary, a treasurer, and sometimes others. The lodge chief appoints a chairman for each lodge committee, both permanent operating committees and temporary committees created from time to time. Chapters have a similar structure. Adults serve as advisers to each youth position as described under "The Scouter's Role," found later in this chapter.

Check with a lodge or chapter officer for more information about your lodge's program. Get together with other Arrowmen in your troop and nearby troops to arrange for transportation.

Your lodge has annual dues that pay for mailing newsletters, annual registration of the lodge, and other necessary lodge expenses. Your first year's dues were probably included in your Ordeal fee. The lodge newsletter will remind you each year of your annual dues and may allow you to pay by mail. You may also be able to pay at lodge activities or at your council service center.

Your lodge has formal, written rules that give the details of its structure. They usually specify offices, operating committees, lodge dues, and makeup of the executive committee. Following the rules, the lodge executive committee plans and carries out the lodge program. The entire lodge may vote on major decisions.

You may expect to receive several issues of your lodge newsletter a year. Rather than mailing at even intervals, lodges tend to send out newsletters before activities. However, if you haven't received anything in 4 months, you may not be on the mailing list. Check with any chapter or lodge officer or the council service center. Because meetings of the entire lodge membership are infrequent, lodge records are much more difficult to maintain properly than troop records.

Lodge (or chapter) events each year include one or more Ordeals, some weekends of service, fun, and fellowship, and perhaps an annual banquet. Most weekends include an opportunity for you to complete Brotherhood membership.

## Service in the Lodge Program

You are invited and encouraged to participate in lodge meetings and projects. The lodge has opportunities for additional service in many areas, some of which are listed here:

• Camping promotion visits to troops and posts

• Publishing a "Where to Go Camping" booklet

• Weekend camp improvement projects

• Sponsorship of Junior Leader Training programs

• Conducting Order of the Arrow elections in units

• Conducting campfires and calling-out ceremonies

Your participation in lodge activities will help you become acquainted with a project or committee in which you can serve actively as a Brotherhood member.

**Committees.** The lodge administers the Order of the Arrow program within the local council. To get the work done, the lodge is organized into committees. Suggested committees are: service, finance, unit elections, ceremonial, membership, and camping promotion. Lodge activity depends on the enthusiastic service of its members. Therefore, the lodge should seek to make committee work interesting and see to it that members are invited to serve on committees that interest them and that committee meetings are held at convenient times and places.

**The method of the Order.** Since the earliest days of the Order, its officers and committees have made decisions based on sound methods of operation. You have read many of these earlier, but they are all here for your review. How have these methods affected your experience with the Order? How can you use them if you become more active in the Order?

• Importance of the individual. The Ordeal accomplishes its purpose through the individual actions of each Arrowman. Each Brother's spiritual and moral values, especially as stated in the Scout Oath and Law, are at the heart of his experience in the Order.

• Importance of camping. The outdoor program of Scouting produces self-reliant citizens. Arrowmen work toward more Scouts camping and having a better experience.

• Setting the example. Qualities of character, like brotherhood, cheerfulness, and service, are hard to understand in the abstract. They come easier when seen in human life. Each Arrowman's example is the main service of the Order to Scouting.

• Induction sequence. Introduction to the principles of the Order occurs in an orderly manner over several months. Each Arrowman grows through a similar pattern of ceremonies, service, and reflection.

• Role of ceremony. Ceremonies present the principles of the Order in an exciting and impressive atmosphere. They enable the members to be more effective in setting the example.

• Role of mystery. Arrowmen maintain an air of mystery about the Order and its ceremonies because of the attractive role mystery plays. To maintain mystery, the Order restricts the pre-Ordeal and Ordeal ceremonies to candidates and members. Other ceremonies of the Order are conducted the same way. However, concerned adults may easily learn about the Order through the lodge staff adviser.

- Democratic selection of members. Full membership in the Order is an honor granted to a Scout by those who know him the best, the Scouts of his troop. All Scouts in the troop may vote in this election.

- Forward looking. Membership in the Order is not given for past accomplishments. Scouting expects each Arrowman to continue his growth and service.

- Equality of membership. Lodge membership entitles an Arrowman to all its rights and privileges.

- Operation of program by youth. Members under 21 plan and operate the program of the lodge. Members 21 and older may not vote. The Scout executive appoints adults as advisers and as supreme chief of the fire has ultimate authority.

- Democratic internal operation. Lodge rules, adopted by the lodge youth membership, govern its affairs. Following these rules, officers are elected by vote of these members.

- Part of the Boy Scouts of America. The Order of the Arrow has no existence apart from Scouting. It is a device used in Scouting's camping program. The lodge is part of the local council and under the administrative authority of the Scout executive. Registered membership in the Boy Scouts of America is a requirement for membership in the Order.

**Section, regional, and national organization.** The Order of the Arrow is fully integrated into the outdoor program of the Boy Scouts of America as the official honor campers' brotherhood. The organization of the Order above the lodge level exists to support the lodge.

Lodges within a geographic area are grouped together to form a section. The section is responsible for organizing and conducting an annual event called *section conclave*, of which training is a major part. The section serves as the link between the lodges in the section and the regional and national offices. The conclaves are organized and directed by youth younger than 21 years of age with support and guidance from selected adults. Each section elects a chief, vice chief, and secretary.

The Boy Scouts of America is organized into six geographic regions. Like the lodge, each region has a Key 3—the region chief (a youth elected by the section chiefs), an OA chairman (a volunteer), and a staff adviser (a regional professional Scouter).

Nationally, the magnitude and dynamics of the Order of the Arrow program require administration by a full-time paid staff—including a director who serves as national staff adviser—headquartered at the BSA's national office and a national committee of dedicated volunteer

Scouters. The Order has a national chief and vice chief, both youth, elected by section chiefs attending the national planning meeting. Both serve as youth members of the national committee composed of approximately 40 people.

Because of the size and complexity of the program and the national committee, a steering committee of national vice chairmen was created to manage the daily and periodic affairs of the Order. The steering committee is composed of the national director, national chairman, immediate past national chairman, national vice chairmen, Founders' Advisory Council chairman, national chief, and national vice chief.

Every 2 years, during the month of August, the Order of the Arrow holds a national conference on the campus of a major university. The conference program includes innovative training sessions, fellowship periods, ceremony competitions, Indian pageants, and camping promotions, displays, and opportunities to hear and to talk to national OA leaders.

Learn more about the Order and its programs by reading the *Order of the Arrow Guide for Officers and Advisers,* No. 4999.

**Dividing the tasks.** The division of labor between lodge officers and committees varies widely. Here is a typical split to suggest how and where you might participate.

What lodges typically do:

• Make long-range plans, including budgets

• Make operating policy decisions

• Keep membership and financial records

• Collect dues; order and sell supplies

• Develop camp promotions and unit elections materials

• Lead participation in sectional and national events

• Publish a lodge bulletin

• Make Vigil Honor nominations and handle other awards

• Provide training

• Plan, run, and evaluate some activities

• Provide liaison to the local council

What chapters typically do:

• Supervise Order of the Arrow elections in the geographical area

- Holds several meetings each year
- Act as a rallying point for members going to lodge activities
- Support a specialized part of the lodge program (such as a ceremonial or dance team)
- Have specific jobs at lodge activities, such as cooking and cleanup, etc.
- Write for the lodge newsletter or its own newsletter

A good chapter does one or two of these each year:

- Conduct a service project
- Provide support at a camporee or Scoutorama
- Perform Indian dances and conduct ceremonies for Cub Scout packs
- Have a callout ceremony

In some large lodges, chapters are like "mini-lodges" and may do the following:

- Hold one or more Ordeals a year
- Hold one or more Brotherhood ceremonies a year

**Camping promotion.** Since the Order of the Arrow is the honor campers brotherhood of the Boy Scouts of America, a lodge's basic objective is to promote the camping program of the local council. This should include troop visitation by members of the lodge or chapter camping promotion committee. Each Arrowman should become the camping promoter in his own unit.

**Proper uniforms.** As a pacesetter in Scouting, each Arrowman should set the example by properly wearing the Scout or Explorer uniform at all Scouting functions.

**Your lodge and the local council.** Your lodge serves as an important part of your local council operation. It aids the council not only with the camping program, but with camp improvement projects and general service to the council when needed.

The lodge works with the council camping committee in coordinating its yearly projects and activities. It is recommended that one of the lodge officers sit on the council camping committee to keep open the lines of communication. The lodge adviser should serve as a member of the camping committee to coordinate the annual programs of the lodge with the objectives of the committee. The Scout executive appoints the lodge and chapter advisers annually. He may, if he chooses, secure the lodge chief's recommendation.

**Lodge membership.** Members of the Order of the Arrow may be official dues-paying (and in the case of youth, voting) members of only one lodge, that being the lodge chartered to the council where they reside and have their principal Scouting registration.

It is acceptable for an Arrowman to maintain contact with a lodge where he was formerly a member, and he is welcome to pay a fee to receive communication from his former lodge if that lodge so permits. However, this former member of the lodge cannot vote and should not attempt to influence lodge policy inasmuch as he is a guest or visitor, not an official dues-paying member of the lodge. He must not attempt to influence lodge policy and cannot vote or hold any office or position.

Arrowmen with extended residence away from their normal home, such as students living away from home at school or members of the military, may maintain their Order of the Arrow membership in either place, but not both. If an Arrowman desires to join the lodge away from home, he must also register in the BSA council at that location. The Order is an integral part of Scouting, and we all owe primary responsibility to Scouting wherever we are members of the Order.

# Brotherhood Membership

From the beginning of the Order in 1915, all members have been equal. There are no ranks. As an Ordeal member you are entitled to all the rights and privileges of membership in the Order. Yet, so important is the induction sequence that the Order strengthened it by creating Brotherhood membership. It is an opportunity for members to evaluate their past service to Scouting (camping and unit involvement) and to the lodge since their Ordeal induction. Brotherhood membership is sought by Arrowmen seeking to reaffirm their belief in the high purposes of the Order. Before becoming a Brotherhood member, each Arrowman makes a special effort to serve his troop and to learn about the Order. Each Brotherhood member commits himself to even more service to Scouting through the Order.

Completing your Ordeal set you on the next part of your "long and toilsome journey," applying what you learned in your Ordeal to your life. When you have learned about the ideals of the Order and made them a part of your life, you may become a Brotherhood member. Brotherhood membership marks the completion of your induction into the Order of the Arrow.

Except for making the necessary arrangements for Brotherhood ceremonies, it is not necessary for Brotherhood members to meet as a separate group. Social and service activities are not held for Brotherhood members apart from other members of the lodge.

The Ordeal, with its tests and ceremonies, presents many ideas and ideals. During the months that follow, you think about your Ordeal. Practicing the principles taught in the Ordeal deepens your understanding of them. Each new experience strengthens your commitment to the Order's principles and purposes. Finally, you are able to accept the additional obligations and insights of the Brotherhood.

Your primary obligation as an Ordeal member is to serve your troop, and only after you are satisfied that you are doing this are you ready for more. The Brotherhood obligation includes a pledge to support the work of the Order. As an Ordeal member, you are invited and encouraged to serve in lodge activities, but you have no obligation to do so. As you approach Brotherhood membership, you should develop a definite idea of how you can serve the Order.

Your Ordeal consisted primarily of physical impressions. The Brotherhood ceremony is one of deeper and quieter mental impressions.

To prepare yourself for Brotherhood membership, refer to the section titled "On the Trail to Brotherhood," immediately following the explanation of the Vigil Honor.

# Vigil Honor

Alertness to the needs of others is the mark of the Vigil Honor. It calls for an individual with an unusual awareness of the possibilities within each situation.

The Vigil Honor is a high mark of distinction and recognition reserved for those Arrowmen who, by reason of exceptional service, personal effort, and unselfish interest, have made distinguished contributions beyond the immediate responsibilities of their position or office to one or more of the following: their lodge, the Order of the Arrow, Scouting, or their Scout camp. Under no circumstances should tenure in Scouting or the Order of the Arrow be considered as reason enough for a Vigil Honor recommendation.

The Vigil Honor is the highest honor that the Order of the Arrow can bestow upon its members for service to lodge, council, and Scouting. It dates from the year 1915, when founder E. Urner Goodman became the first Vigil Honor member. Since then, thousands of members have been given this honor.

Vigil Honor members have an honorable tradition to uphold. They must at all times conduct themselves in accordance with the ideals of

Scouting, the Order of the Arrow, and the Vigil Honor. Membership cannot be won by a person's conscious endeavor. It comes as a recognition of his unselfish leadership in service. This fact should be given careful consideration in the selection of candidates for membership. The Vigil Honor has successfully fulfilled a definite and satisfactory service to the Order of the Arrow, to Scouting, and to individual members. Its continued success depends on the care with which future members are selected and on the maintenance by its members of the high ideals of service to others for which the Vigil Honor has always been known.

Any member of the Order of the Arrow registered in Scouting and in good standing in a regularly chartered lodge is eligible for recommendation to the national Order of the Arrow Committee for elevation to the Vigil Honor, provided that, at the time of his recommendation, he has been a Brotherhood member for a minimum of 2 years. Because the Order of the Arrow is primarily an organization for youth, it is suggested that, in recommending candidates for the Vigil Honor, preference be given to those who became members of the Order as Scouts rather than to those who were inducted into the Order as adult volunteer or professional Scouters.

Members of the Order can be inducted into the Vigil Honor only with the written approval of the national Order of the Arrow committee.

# On the Trail to Brotherhood

Your completion of the Ordeal sets you on the start of an exciting adventure. After at least 10 months of active service you will be eligible to seal your membership in the Brotherhood ceremony.

The Ordeal has introduced you to the mysteries of the Order. Now, during your service as an Ordeal member, you have ample opportunity to increase your knowledge of the Arrow and to make it work for you.

This handbook provides all the basic information you will need during this important time. Your brothers in the Order stand ready to help also, and you should take advantage of their support whenever possible.

## The Challenges of Brotherhood Membership

You must meet five challenges before you can enter the Circle of the Brotherhood. The first of these you should meet now. The next three require steady effort over a period of months. The last challenge you must meet after you are satisfied that you are meeting the first four.

1. **Memorize the signs of Arrow membership.** Memorize the Obligation of the Order, which you received from Allowat Sakima (printed on the back of your membership card and in your handbook). Also, memorize the Order of the Arrow Official Song, the Admonition, the sign of Ordeal membership, and the Arrow handclasp.

2. **Advance in your understanding of the Ordeal.** Gain a thorough understanding of the Ordeal through which you have passed.

3. **Serve your unit.** Retain your registration in Scouting. During a period of at least 10 months, strive to fulfill your Obligation by continuing and expanding your service to your own troop, team, or post.

4. **Plan for service in your lodge.** Retain your registration in your Order of the Arrow lodge and keep your dues paid. Be aware that acceptance of Brotherhood membership involves a pledge of service to the lodge. Develop a concrete idea of how you plan to fulfill this pledge.

5. **Review your progress.** When you earnestly feel that you have met the four challenges above, write a letter to your lodge secretary. In this letter:

   • Explain what you think the Obligation means.

   • Describe how you have been fulfilling this Obligation in your troop or post and in your daily life, and how you have used your understanding of the Ordeal to aid in this service.

   • Describe your specific plans for giving service in the lodge program.

   Include with this letter your advance registration application and fees for the next Brotherhood ceremony according to the instructions given by the lodge.

**Your life as a Brotherhood member.** Brotherhood members have pledged to serve the Order. This service takes many forms. Your Scoutmaster encourages you on, speaks well of the lodge, and gets you a ride to Order of the Arrow events. He's serving the Order. Another Scout in your troop gives camp promotion talks in neighboring troops. Still another Brother is training to be an Elangomat at the next Ordeal.

Your junior assistant Scoutmaster is unit elections chairman. An assistant Scoutmaster is a carpenter. He takes his tools with him to camp whenever he goes and helps the camp ranger with odd jobs. All are serving the Order, each in his own way; each as his other commitments permit.

As a Brotherhood member your first responsibility in Scouting is still your troop. Your Scoutmaster relies on your example, as an older, more experienced Scout; on your willingness to teach; on your leadership. Yet as a Brotherhood member you want to take on more responsibilities in the Order. How do you reconcile this with your responsibility to your troop?

Before assuming any new task, discuss it with your Scoutmaster. Together, determine how it affects your troop life. When your Scoutmaster knows you are working for Scouting outside your troop he can better help you plan your activities within the troop.

Start by limiting yourself to responsibilities that will not conflict with your troop. For example, agree to do elections for new members only on nights when your troop doesn't meet. If you eventually choose to assume a leadership role in the Order, recognize that you will have less time to spend with your troop. As a chapter or lodge officer, you will have to plan around the needs of all the Brothers, not just your own.

As you plan your service to the Order, you will want to do three things. Find ways to get involved. Understand your own needs and desires. Remember, there are many ways to serve in the Order. You will be most successful as a Brotherhood member if you match your service to your needs. Finally, if you have the opportunity, discuss possible service with a lodge or chapter officer. He will cheerfully show you many ways to serve.

The Order of the Arrow is a service organization. It serves Scouting by promoting the Scout Oath and Law and especially the principles of brotherhood, cheerfulness, and service. It serves Scouting by promoting Scout camping and by building and maintaining camping traditions. It serves Scouting by turning your habit of a Good Turn daily into a lifetime purpose of leadership in cheerful service.

Yet the Order is not some machine or strange beast. The Order is the Brothers who strive to fulfill its Obligation, and you are a Brother. When your example promotes the principles, when your help to a fellow Scout makes him a better camper, when your daily Good Turn becomes a life of leadership in service, when you remember the Admonition, you are the Order.

# The Customs and Traditions of the Ordeal

## Questions and Answers

**Q.** Who is Kichkinet? Nutiket? Meteu? Allowat Sakima?

**A.** Kichkinet is your guide in the ceremonies. He symbolizes helpfulness and friendliness. Nutiket is the guard of the Circle. He upholds the tradition of cheerfulness. Meteu is the medicine man and representative of brotherhood. He reminds us of our need to love one another. Allowat Sakima, the mighty chief, symbolizes service. From him you accepted the Obligation of the Order.

**Q.** What tokens did the four ceremonial principals reveal to you in the pre-Ordeal, and what did they represent?

**A.** Nutiket gave the bow to Allowat Sakima as a token of liveliness and flexibility under stress, the principle of cheerfulness. Meteu gave the bowstring to Allowat Sakima as a token of the ties of Brotherhood also symbolized by the rope in the Ordeal ceremony. Allowat Sakima strung the bow uniting brotherhood and cheerfulness for service, and drew an arrow from a quiver as a token that your election separated you from your fellows for something higher. Allowat Sakima asked you to test the bow as a sign of willingness to test the dedication to Scout ideals which led to your election. Lastly, Kichkinet shot the arrow upward, symbolizing the pathway you will follow if your dedication is unwavering.

**Q.** What are the tests of the Ordeal, and what do they illustrate?

**A.** The night alone focuses attention on your need for courage and self-reliance on the trail ahead. You must be willing to accept individual responsibility for your thoughts and actions. You will find that your course will set you apart from your friends to the extent of isolation, but you must act according to your resolution regardless of what others do or fail to do.

Your pledge of silence emphasizes the continuing need for you to spend time in thoughtful silence. Difficult decisions will face you now and in the future, and you will need to search your heart and spirit deeply to find the resolution that will guide you onward successfully.

The scant food test illustrates self-denial. Often you will find it necessary to abandon mere personal comfort or desires if you are to fulfill your Obligation.

The day of work indicates your willingness to give service, even when this service involves hardship and toil. In the Ordeal, you worked with the help and cooperation of other candidates and members, but now you must be ready to serve without the help and cooperation of others.

**Q. What are the three symbolic preparations for the Obligation?**

A. Before you entered the circle, you placed your hand on the shoulder of the candidate ahead of you to indicate your intention to continue in service to your own Scout or Explorer unit. Kichkinet, seeing that you all had the same purpose, symbolized this bond of brotherhood by binding you all together with the rope. Finally, upon Allowat Sakima's direction, Kichkinet asked you to advance before the fire of cheerfulness.

**Q. What is the tradition given us by Uncas as described in the legend?**

A. The legend tells how the peaceful lives of the Lenni-Lenape Indians were threatened by neighboring tribes and distant enemies. Chief Chingachgook's call for volunteers to go and alert other villages of the tribe was met with apathy and indifference from tribal members. Uncas cheerfully offered his help despite the negative attitudes of everyone around him. He cared enough for others that he was willing to face hardship and danger to protect them from harm. Uncas clearly saw a higher vision, and his desire for his brothers was that they could see it, too. The self-sacrificing service given by Uncas and Chingachgook is said to have saved the tribe from annihilation.

**Q. What is the significance of Allowat Sakima's description of the Arrow in the Ordeal ceremony?**

A. The chief stated that the various qualities attributed to the Arrow are ingredients of leadership. His discussion is a continuation of Meteu's comments about the Arrow in the pre-Ordeal. The Ordeal asks each one to act according to his highest sense of right, regardless of the attitudes or actions of others. The four tests and the Obligation point the way, and Allowat Sakima reveals this way as one of real leadership. Any member who understands his Obligation and is striving to fulfill it inevitably becomes a center of strength in his troop or post. His example sets the pace in cheerful service, and his dedication has a rich effect on those who know him. Although wearing the sash identifies a Scout as a member of the Order, it is his efforts to fulfill his Obligation that truly distinguishes him and provides others with glimpses of the Arrow.

**Q. What is Ordeal membership?**

A. Like the Ordeal, it is a time of trial, during which your understanding of the traditions of the Arrow will be put to the test. In the Ordeal ceremony, each advancement you made into the circle was challenged, but your resolution and faithfulness in time of testing enabled you to go forward. You will find this to be true also in the experiences ahead. By striving to fulfill your Obligation, you will provide the higher vision of Brotherhood, Cheerfulness, and Service to your fellow Scouts or Explorers, even as Uncas did for his tribe.

**Q. When are you ready to accept Brotherhood membership in the Order?**

A. Successfully meeting the demands of the Obligation is usually rather hard for the first several months. Gradually, however, your dedication to it will bring about changes that will make it easier for you. Eventually, the Spirit of Cheerful Service will become almost second nature to you, and you will be fulfilling the Obligation and hardly even thinking about it. As this experience develops, you are beginning to see the Arrow, and you are ready for the Brotherhood.

# Future Service for Arrowmen

In addition to service, fellowship, and fun during the years of membership in the Order of the Arrow, there are many opportunities for service that Arrowmen can look forward to in the future. The lessons learned in Scouting, Exploring, and in the Order are of great value in preparing for positions of leadership in tomorrow's world. Cheerful service to our fellowmen often becomes a lifelong habit. As members of the lodge mature and take their places in adult society, they will find the following ways to continue their interests in Scouting and service.

**Alpha Phi Omega.** This is a national service fraternity for college and university students, founded in 1925 and now active on more than 450 campuses in the United States. Its purpose is to assemble college students in the fellowship of the principles of the Boy Scouts of America as embodied in its Scout Oath and Law, to develop leadership; to promote friendship; to provide service to humanity; and to further the freedom that is our national, educational, and intellectual heritage.

Arrowmen interested in membership in this fraternity may write for detailed information. The address is the National Alpha Phi Omega Office, 400 Mainmark Building, 1627 Main Street, Kansas City, MO 64106.

**The National Eagle Scout Association.** Eagle Scouts may join the National Eagle Scout Association. Many local councils have active chapters on both a formal and informal basis. It's a fine way to give active service to Scouting. Contact your council service center for more information.

**College Scouter Reserve.** Arrowmen unable to continue active unit service while in college may continue their registration with the Boy Scouts of America by joining the College Scouter Reserve. This will permit them to maintain their membership in an Order of the Arrow lodge. Applications are available through the local council service center.

**Volunteer leadership in Scouting.** The growth of Scouting depends upon capable, dedicated volunteer leadership. Most Arrowmen have the know-how and leadership capabilities needed in Scouting leadership today.

Volunteer leadership positions in Scouting present a challenging opportunity. Councils are continually in need of qualified individuals to serve as unit leaders, unit committee members, commissioners, merit badge counselors, and in other positions in the district and council. Arrowmen serving in any leadership capacity can continue their active membership in an Order of the Arrow lodge.

Volunteer service in Scouting can become a lifelong interest and a fascinating hobby that fulfills one of the highest callings of good citizenship. A great many of the Cubmasters, Scoutmasters, Varsity Scout Coaches, Explorer Advisors, and their associates who will lead units are now active members of the Order of the Arrow.

"He alone is worthy to wear the arrow who will continue faithfully to serve his fellow man."

**Professional Scouting.** Arrowmen who have a definite desire to serve others should consider professional Scouting as a career.

Scouting is the largest voluntary youth organization in the free world today. As Scouting continues to grow, there is an opportunity each year for more than 1,000 individuals to join its ever-expanding professional ranks.

Your Scout executive or a member of the executive staff will be glad to talk with you about career opportunities with the Boy Scouts of America. Arrowmen seriously considering professional Scouting should continue unit service and their membership in the Order of the Arrow during college.

# Uniform and Insignia

The official insignia of the Order of the Arrow are some of the most colorful in Scouting. It is the responsibility of all Arrowmen to wear them proudly and correctly.

Only currently registered members of the Boy Scouts of America and the Order may wear the insignia of the Order of the Arrow.

An explanation of the various insignia is included below.

**Arrow sashes.** The official Order of the Arrow sash is available for members through the lodge or local council service center, or through the Supply Division of the Boy Scouts of America. It is a white fabric sash with a red arrow embroidered upon it.

Ordeal members wear the sash with a red embroidered arrow. Brotherhood members wear the sash with a red embroidered arrow enclosed by two red bars.

Vigil Honor members alone wear the sash with a red embroidered arrow enclosed between two red bars, bearing a red triangle superimposed on the arrow shaft. Contained within the red triangle are three white arrows.

The Order of the Arrow sash is worn with official "Class A" uniform or Scouting's official adult dress wear (a blue blazer and gray slacks). The sash also may be worn by Elangomats who are not in "Class A" uniform at an Ordeal, youth wearing ceremonial attire, and in such other instances as approved by the Scout executive. The sash is worn over the right shoulder and, if in "Class A" uniform, *under* the shoulder loop (or epaulet) so that the arrow is pointing over the right shoulder. The sash is worn diagonally across the chest. It is not to be worn in any other manner.

Sashes may not be altered in any way or form. Beading or any other material is not permitted on the sash. Nothing is to be worn on the sash, including signatures, patches of any kind, pins, or legends. The only exceptions are the 50th and 60th anniversary awards. These may be worn as an option, for those who have earned them, on the shoulder portion above the bar at the point of the arrow.

The sash is worn at Order of the Arrow functions and special Scouting activities, including courts of honor and on occasions when members need to be identified as Arrowmen rendering special services.

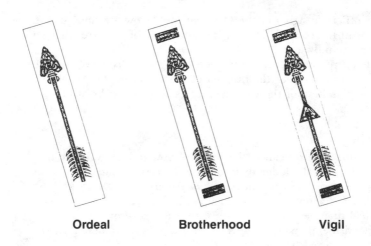

**Ordeal**          **Brotherhood**          **Vigil**

**Lodge pocket flap.** Cloth lodge emblems ("flaps") are made available by most lodges. National policy requires that these pocket flap patches be made of, and embroidered on, cloth, and must be of a size and shape so as to cover the right breast pocket flap and not extend beyond the outer edge of the uniform pocket flap. They usually show the lodge name and totem.

Beading of flaps is against uniform and insignia policy. The national Order of the Arrow Committee recommends that no restrictions be placed on the purchase of lodge flap patches.

**Universal Arrow ribbon.** The Universal Arrow badge is a silver arrow suspended from a red-and-white ribbon. It is worn hanging from the button of the right breast pocket of the uniform shirt. It is to be worn only with the official Scout uniform.

**Universal Arrow Ribbon**

**Founders' Award ribbon.** Recipients of the Founders' Award are entitled to wear the Founders' Award ribbon, which is similar to the Universal Arrow ribbon, except that it is a gold-colored arrow suspended from a red ribbon.

**Vigil Honor recognition.** The red-and-white universal ribbon with centered and attached Vigil Honor pin is worn by Vigil Honor members only.

**Vigil Honor Pin**

**Distinguished Service Award square knot.** An embroidered cloth knot (white knot on red cloth) is available for holders of the Order's National Distinguished Service Award. The knot is worn as prescribed in the BSA *Insignia Guide.*

**Distinguished Service Award Square Knot**

**Shoulder loops (epaulets).** Colored shoulder loops identify the area of Scouting in which a member has his primary paid registered position. The loops approved for uniform use are: blue, Cub Scouting; red, Boy Scouting; blaze, Varsity Scouting; green, Exploring; silver, council or district registration; gold, national and regional registration.

Members should not change loop colors because of Order of the Arrow participation or position, unless it is representative of the Arrowman's paid registration. For example, a lodge adviser would wear silver loops only if he is registered in that capacity, which is a council level registration, or some other council level capacity; a section chief would wear loops depicting his registration, which would be on a council or unit level, as section office is not a registered position.

**Civilian Arrow pins.** The Arrow pins are for nonuniform wear. This simple silver lapel pin may be worn by all members of the Order.

**Adviser's badge of office.** A special adviser's patch is available for section, lodge, and chapter advisers. It is to be worn on the left sleeve of the uniform in a location prescribed for badge of office. These badges of office are the only badges authorized for Arrow positions.

**Patch collecting.** Patch collecting and trading is as old as Scouting. Millions of Scouts have found patch trading a unique hobby, equally as exciting as collecting stamps or coins are to philatelists and numismatists.

Principles of fair play must always dominate every patch trading experience. Money must never be exchanged as part of patch trading. No high-pressure tactics should ever be involved. You may find that Arrow events have specifically scheduled hours, times, or locations for patch trading. You should conform to these standards. The BSA regulation regarding badge swapping is as follows (from the *Insignia Control Guide*):

"Boy Scouts and Explorers attending jamborees may swap among themselves articles and novelties of a local or regional nature. The swapping of such items as badges of office, rank, distinguished service, training, performance, achievement, and distinction, however, is a violation of Article X of the *Rules and Regulations of the Boy Scouts of America*, forbidding the holding of these badges by any but the members who have complied with the requirements for them."

## The Scouter's Role

The role of the adult Scouter in the Order of the Arrow is the same as it is throughout Scouting. Scouters help young men grow through a program the youth plan and run. This help includes training, counseling, and advising leaders and sometimes counseling individual members.

There are, however, some practical differences. In the troop, there are fewer adult leaders than boy leaders, so each Scouter is kept busy advising several Scouts. On the other hand, at Order of the Arrow events there are far more Scouters present than elected lodge leaders. Thus, most Scouters in the Order must take a back-seat role, lending support for those who attend Order functions, but without a direct advisory relationship to any leader.

As a Scouter, you wear the Arrow to make it more significant to Scouts. If you were elected as an adult, it was for this reason, rather than as an honor or award. Nonetheless, your own induction into the Order is your opportunity for personal growth. Further, you are observed by younger Arrowmen and must be an exemplary participant.

A note of caution: If you were an active Arrowman as a youth, you have the special challenge of learning new leadership styles. No longer will you be planning, voting, leading. Now you have far greater joys as you watch the young men achieve their successes.

There are two distinct Scouter roles in the Order: that of the adviser appointed for a particular youth leader, and that of other Scouters.

**Role of the adviser in the Order.** Each chapter or lodge officer or committee chairman has an appointed adviser. Officers in the Order are elected by the youth members, and the officers appoint committee chairmen. Advisers are appointed by the Scout executive, usually for the same term as the officers. The Scout executive, as the lodge's Supreme Chief of the Fire, is the highest adviser in the lodge.

Each adviser in the Order provides support for the program to which he has been assigned. It is inappropriate for an adviser to run the program, although he should always be involved. It is the adviser's task to make sure that the young men succeed. This includes training, transportation, and staying constantly involved and informed.

The proper role of an adviser is the same as the proper role of a Scoutmaster. An adviser works almost completely behind the scenes. Although the Order's program is more complex than a troop's, the leaders in the Order are older and more experienced. Yet, they still benefit from sound guidance and enthusiastic support. Watching outstanding leaders succeed is one of the most enjoyable parts of being an adviser.

**Role of the nonadviser Scouter.** As a Scouter without an adviser appointment, your main responsibility in Scouting lies outside the Order of the Arrow. Your main duty within the Order is to support its program in your Scouting position.

If you serve as Scoutmaster, you know that your attitudes will be reflected in those of your Scouts. You may not have the time to attend Order activities regularly. Troop functions, roundtables, and Scout leader training come first. But you can make your feelings toward the Order known. Since you understand the importance of your troop to the Order, you can speak well of it. As a result your Scouts will support both. Since your time is limited, encourage one of your assistants who is an Arrowman to make the Order his special responsibility. Your Arrowmen will then have a source of transportation and an additional source of inspiration.

Many Scouters find Order of the Arrow functions an excellent opportunity to relax, take stock, meet other Scouters, and get to know their youth leaders better. Your efforts to support the Arrow during these activities will be appreciated. Offer transportation or help with a special skill. But especially give your positive example and encouragement to all Brothers.

# Indian Customs and Traditions

A fascinating feature of the Order of the Arrow is its wide use of Indian lore, customs, and attire. Indian lore, Indian attire, and terminology are not the main themes of the Order, but they are an exciting part of the program.

Many young men are interested in the history, traditions, and customs of native Americans. This study, as a by-product of the program, has become a popular hobby for many youth and adults who first became aware of Indian lore through their Order of the Arrow membership.

Your first exposure to this was probably in viewing the ceremonial team, with its four principle members: Allowat Sakima, the mighty chief; Meteu, the medicine man; Nutiket, the guard; Kichkinet, the guide.

**Pronunciation of key words.** Here is a simple guide to help you with pronunciation of Indian words you will often hear.

## In the Legend

| | | |
|---|---|---|
| The Delaware Indians | Lenni Lenape | Len'nee Len-ah'pee |
| The Chieftain | Chingachgook | Ching'gatch-gook |
| The Chieftain's son | Uncas | Un'cuss |

## The Principles and Full Name of the Order

| | | |
|---|---|---|
| Brotherhood | Wimachtendienk | Wee-mok'ten-dee-enk |
| Cheerfulness | Wingolauchsik | Win'go-lough-sik |
| Service | Witahemui | Wi'tah-hem'oo-ee |

## The Ceremonial Figures

| | | |
|---|---|---|
| Mighty Chief | Allowat Sakima | Al'lo-wot Sa-kee'ma |
| Medicine Man | Meteu | Mee-tay'o |
| The Guard | Nutiket | Nu-te'ket |
| The Guide | Kichkinet | Kitch'kin-et |

**Initial understanding.** Each Indian tribe is different. Hollywood portrays Indians wearing feathered headdresses and beadwork patterns, living in tepees, and riding horses. Yet many tribes never had these customs. Some of these practices did not exist until introduced by Europeans. Many aspects of the plains Indian cultures did not exist before the arrival of the horse with the Spanish. What we call American Indian beadwork is made of manufactured glass beads, as were traded to native Americans by Europeans. Handmade beads were not worn in large patterns on clothing because of the work it took to make each bead. Still, beadwork is a genuine American Indian craft.

Know the historical and geographical context of a particular practice. Native American cultures were not static even before European settlement, and changed after European contact. Even before the 1500s, lifestyles differed markedly across the hemisphere. Peoples separated by only several hundred miles had very different lifestyles. Without such understanding, your attempts to honor and spread knowledge of Indian culture may do exactly the opposite.

Specialize to gain understanding. A smattering of learning about more than 200 tribes or nations gains you little. Deep study of a single one of the widely differing groups will give you a sincere appreciation of their way of life.

Choose a tribe that does or did live locally, since more material will be available to you. The best place to start is at the library. Use the card catalog to make a list of everything available about the tribe. As you read the cards in the subject catalog, be on alert for tribal names. The name you apply to the tribe may not have been what they called themselves. (It might be a derisive term applied by neighboring enemies.) Thus, one tribe may be given several names, or, even more confusing, the same name may be applied to several groups of people.

Most tribes consisted simply of those people who spoke the same language. Europeans treated an Indian tribe as a small cohesive country. Yet some did not have strong political structures above the village level. Even social structures, such as annual festivals, varied somewhat from group to group within a single people.


**Reading and research.** Use your list to start with the books that will be best for you. There are three distinct kinds of literature on Indian lore. First, there are popularizations such as the books by Ben Hunt. These are valuable for getting people interested in Indian culture, and may contain some practical material on Indian crafts. But the details are often not authentic. If the author does not give the tribe, geographical location, and historical era, consider it suspect.

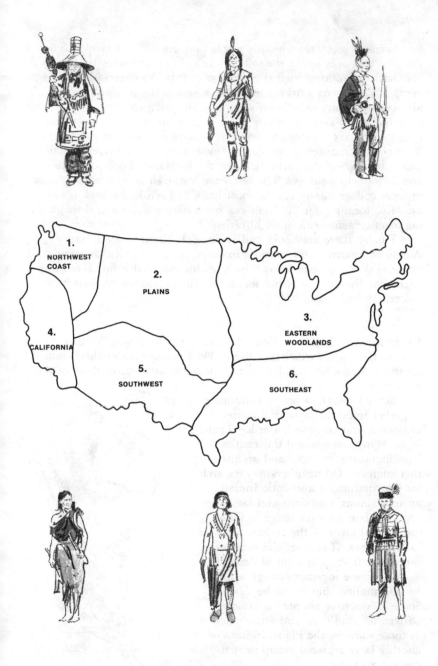

1. NORTHWEST COAST

2. PLAINS

3. EASTERN WOODLANDS

4. CALIFORNIA

5. SOUTHWEST

6. SOUTHEAST

Second, there are scholarly works that are archeological (studies of the past by traces left in the soil), historical (written records of early contacts), or anthropological (studies of culture by observation and interview). The primary works—those which report the original research—are scientific journals, scholarly reports, and monographs. Many of these were sponsored and printed by the U.S. government. Scholars summarize the primary sources and rework the data into surveys and textbooks. Textbooks introduce the subject to a newcomer, while surveys usually tour some part of the entire field for the specialist. Look for textbooks and introductory surveys. The reference librarian at your school, public, or local college library can be most helpful. Even if the book is not available locally, your librarian can often obtain it for you through sharing arrangements with other libraries.

Finally, there are books and periodicals about modern native American culture. This includes material on ceremonies, dancing, and crafts as they are done today. Much of this material is not about any particular Indian group, but focuses on the major reservations in the western United States.

**Using local Indian traditions.** Lodges are encouraged to study the customs of the Indian tribes that live or lived in the area of their council territory. If possible, a lodge should model its attire after those of the local tribes.

Some lodges have set up committees to gather information from libraries, museums, and ethnologists at local colleges. Many colleges and universities have literature, exhibits, and archives that interested OA members may research for information on authentic Indian attire, customs, traditions and language.

It is best for each lodge to follow the general attire of the Indian tribes of its home area. It may require some extra time and effort, plus a bit of detective work, to piece together enough authentic information, but it can be done. Some lodges have adopted a broader pattern for traditions and attire, such as those worn by the Plains Indians or another large regional group near its council area.

**Indian dances.** A Scout is reverent. Observing the twelfth point of the Scout Law has two equal parts: Doing your duty to God, and respecting the religious beliefs of others. Scouts must even respect beliefs no longer practiced. Many traditional dances of various Indian tribes have religious themes.

We must always remember that a religion belongs to the people practicing it. A nonbeliever cannot perform a sacred dance without degrading or insulting the original religious intent. For this reason, any dance that has religious connotations must be avoided.

You would be offended if your worship service was used for entertainment. Doing a religious Indian dance as a nonbeliever is just as offensive. Religion has a strong role in native American culture. Therefore, learn and respect the difference between the social dances, songs, crafts, and regalia, and those associated with religious practices. Care in this regard will help you appreciate the native American life all the more.

Your lodge should have members who are sensitive to and informed about this issue. Contact these members, work with them, and heed their advice. Then you can honor rather than debase the culture of the true discoverers of America.

The following general rules will assist in recognizing those dances that should be avoided: (1) Dances utilizing a mask, including the use of Katchinas, false faces, Northwest Coast masks, and many others. (2) Pipe ceremonies invoking spirits. (3) Petitions to a higher power, including blessings, thanksgiving prayers for rain, food, or a good harvest. The most abused dance of this type is the Hopi snake dance. These dances should be avoided, even though they may be favored by young dancers who judge the merits of a dance only by the action opportunities it presents.

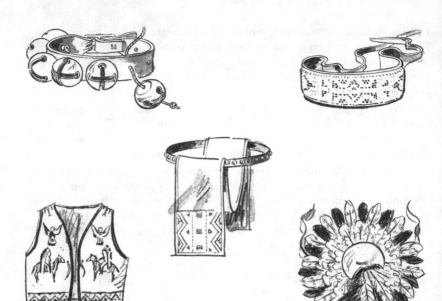

**Indian attire materials.** Many materials for making attire are available to anyone willing to look for them. Much of the fun of making attire is in the gathering of materials: hides and pelts from neighbors who hunt, turkey feathers from a local poultry farm, a raccoon coat or a bearskin rug from an attic. Seek and you may find!

There are Indian crafts suppliers in most parts of our country. Check current issues of *Whispering Wind* for listings.

Try to get as close to the original material as is economically and legally possible. There are many fine substitutes that are usable, although some leather substitutes are more expensive than leather itself. An old navy blue blanket or trade cloth can be used, but should be dry-cleaned and not allowed to get wet. When making cloth leggings, make them in the cloth style. Never use cloth as imitation leather.

Feathers also can be a problem. Your safest bet is imitation eagle feathers made from turkey feathers. There are many state and federal laws protecting endangered birds. Both our native eagles are under the protection of federal laws that prohibit the possession or transfer of eagle feathers from bald eagles killed after June 8, 1940, and from golden eagles killed after October 24, 1962. The law covers all methods of getting new eagle feathers, so stick to the best imitations or substitutions you can get.

**Resource material on Indian lore.** There are literally hundreds of books describing the traditions and customs, attire, body decorations, and ceremonial regalia of the Indians in every part of our country. Some of these books are listed in the bibliography of this handbook.

The bibliography lists more than 100 books, pamphlets, and periodicals about American Indians. These references offer a handy resource for Arrowmen who would like to learn more about the history and culture of the various tribes that first inhabited these lands. Your experience as an Arrowman could lead to a solid background and lifelong interest in this subject.

The bibliography is organized geographically so that you can read about the Indians of your particular area. There also are lists pertaining to Indian attire, crafts, and dances. Following the bibliography is a Lenni Lenape word list that provides a fairly extensive vocabulary for this dialect.

The reference materials may be found at your school or public library. Ask your librarian for other books about Indians. Find out if there are any museums in your community that contain Indian exhibits.

**OA packet from the Museum of the American Indian.** Through special arrangement, the Museum of the American Indian will provide a selection of pamphlets describing the museum and the services it provides. Arrowmen wishing to get these pamphlets should send a note requesting the OA packet with their name and address and $2.00 for handling and materials to Museum of the American Indian, Broadway at 155th Street, New York, NY 10032.

# INDIAN HOBBYIST BIBLIOGRAPHY

## OA Packet from the Museum of the American Indian

Through special arrangement, the Museum of the American Indian will provide a selection of pamphlets describing the museum and the services it provides. Arrowmen wishing to get these pamphlets should send a note requesting the OA Packet with their name and address and $2 for handling and materials to Museum of the American Indian, Broadway at 115th Street, New York, NY 10032.

## Reference Materials

*Annual Reports of the Bureau of American Ethnology*

*Bulletins of the Bureau of American Ethnology*

Chippewa and Dakota Indians—*Subject Catalog of Books, Pamphlets, Periodicals, Manuscripts in the Minnesota Historical Society,* St. Paul, 1969

*Folk Music: A Catalog of Folk Songs, Ballads, Dances, Instrumental Pieces, and Folk Tales of the United States and Latin America on Phonograph Records,* Music Division, Library of Congress, Washington, DC 20540

Freeman and Smith, *A Guide to Manuscripts Relating to the American Indian,* American Philosophical Society, Philadelphia, 1966

Harding, A. D., and Bolling, *Bibliography of the Articles and Papers on the North American Indians,* Kraus Reprint, N.Y. 1969

Haywood, Charles, *A Bibliography of North American Folklore and Folksong, Volume Two: The American Indians North of Mexico, Including the Eskimos,* 1961

Murdock, George P., *Ethnographic Bibliography of North America,* New Haven, 1960

*Official Museum Directory,* American Association of Museums, arranged geographically and indexed by topic, 1971

Rouse, I., and Goggin, *An Anthropological Bibliography of the Eastern Seaboard, ESAF Research Publication No. 1,* New Haven, 1947

Ullom, Judith, *Folklore of the American Indians,* Washington, 1969

# General Information

Boas, Franz, *Primitive Art,* 1962

Brandon, William, *The American Heritage Book of Indians,* illus., 1961

Curtis, Natalie, *The Indian's Book,* 1968

*Denver Art Museum Leaflet Series,* 119 pamphlets, about $15 per set

Dockstader, Frederick J., *Indian Art in America,* 1968

Driver, Harold, *Indians of North America,* 1969

Ewers, John C., *Artists of the Old West,* 1965

Feder, Norman, *American Indian Art,* 1971

LaFarge, Oliver, *The American Indian,* 1960

LaFarge, Oliver, *A Pictorial History of the American Indian,* 1956

McCracken, Harold, *George Catlin and the Old Frontier,* 1959

McKenny, Thomas L., and Hall, James, *Indian Tribes of North America: With Biographical Sketches and Anecdotes on the Principle Chiefs,* 1932 repr. 1970

*Material Culture Notes,* Denver Art Museum, 136 pp.

Miles, Charles, *Indian and Eskimo Artifacts of North America,* 1963

Owen, Roger C., et al., *The North American Indians: A Sourcebook,* 1967

Terrell, John U., *American Indian Almanac,* 1971

# Periodicals

*Akwesasne Notes,* Mohawk Nation, Rooseveltown, 13693; Nine times yearly, 48-page tabloid format with illustrations and photos

*American Indian Art Magazine* (quarterly), 7045 3d Ave., Scottsdale, AZ 85201

*American Indian Crafts and Culture* (formerly *Singing Wire*), AICC, P.O. Box 3538F, Tulsa, OK 74152; 10 issues per year (ceased publication)

*American Indian Tradition* (formerly *American Indian Hobbyist*), ceased publication

*Indian America,* P.O. Box 52038, Tulsa, OK 74152

*The Indian Historian,* The American Indian Historical Society, 1451 Masonic Ave., San Francisco, CA 94117; quarterly

*Powwow Trails,* ceased publication, some back issues from Powwow Trails, P.O. Box 258F, South Plainfield, NJ 07080

*The Weewish Tree,* a magazine of Indian America for young people, The American Indian Historical Society, 1451 Masonic Ave., San Francisco, CA 94117; six times a year

*Whispering Wind* (10 issues/yr.), 8009 Wales, New Orleans, LA 70126

# Key to Abbreviations Used in "Geographical Information"

AA       —*American Anthropoligist,* new series

AMGLS —*American Museum of Natural History Guide Leaflet Series*

APAM   —*Anthropoligical Papers of the American Museum of Natural History*

ARBAE —*Annual Report of the Bureau of American Ethnology*

ARSI — *Annual Report of the Smithsonian Institute*

BBAE — *Bulletin of the Bureau of American Ethnology*

BPMCM — *Bulletin of the Public Museum of the City of Milwaukee*

CMAI — *Contributions From the Museum of the American Indian,* Heye Foundation

INM — *Indian Notes and Monographs,* Museum of the American Indian, Heye Foundation

MCDM — *Memoirs of the Canada Department of Mines, Geological Survey*

OCMA — *Occasional Contributions from the Museum of Anthropology of the University of Michigan*

PAAS — *Proceedings of the American Antiquarian Society*

PMA — *Papers of the Michigan Academy of Science, Arts and letters*

# Geographical Information

## Southeast

Brannon, D. G., "The Dress of the Early Indians of Alabama," *Arrow Points,* pp. 84–92, 1922

Cushman, H. B., *History of the Choctaw, Chickasaw and Natchez Indians,* Greenville, 1899

Foreman, Grant, *The Five Civilized Tribes,* 1971

Fundaburk, Emma L., *Southeastern Indians: Life Portraits,* 1969

Fundaburk, Emma L., *Sun Circles and Human Hands: The Southeastern Indians—Art and Industry,* 1957

McReynolds, E. C., *The Seminoles,* 1967

Swanton, John R., "Indian Tribes of the Lower Mississippi Valley and Adjacent Coast of the Gulf of Mexico," *BBAE*, XLIII, 1911, repr. 1970

Swanton, John R., "Indians of the Southeastern United States," *BBAE*, CXXXVII, 1945, repr. 1970

## Northeast

DeForest, J. W., *History of the Indians of Connecticut*, repr. 1970

Harrington, M. R., *The Indians of New Jersey: Dickon Among the Lenape*, 1963

Lyford, Carrie, *Iroquois Crafts*, 97 pp.

Rainey, F. G., "A Composition of Historical Data Contributing to the Ethnography of Connecticut and Southern New England Indians," *Bulletin of the Archaeological Society of Connecticut*, III, 1–89, 1936

Speck, Frank G., "Notes on the Material Culture of the Huron," *AA*, n.s., XIII, 208–28, 1911

Willoughby, Charles C., "Dress and Ornaments of the New England Indians," *AA*, n.s., VII, 499–508, 1905

Willoughby, Charles C., "Houses and Gardens of the New England Indians," *AA*, n.s., X, 423–34, 1908

## Plains

Blish, Helen, *Pictographic History of the Oglala Sioux*, 1967

Catlin, George, *Letters and Notes on the North American Indians*

Ewers, John C., *Blackfeet Crafts*, 66 pp.

Grinnell, George B., *The Cheyenne Indians: . . .*, 2 vols., 1923

Lowie, Robert H., *Indians of the Plains*, 258 pp.

Powers, William K., *Indians of the Northern Plains*, 1969

Wissler, Clark, *North American Indians of the Plains*, 1941

## California

Heizer, Robert, *Languages, Territories and Names of California Indian Tribes*, 1966

Heizer, Robert, and Whipple, M. A., *The California Indians*, 1951

Kroeber, A. L., "Handbook of the Indians of California," *BBAE*, LXXVIII, 1-995, 1925, repr. 1970

Underhill, Ruth, *Indians of Southern California*, 73 pp.

Underhill, Ruth, *The Northern Paiute Indians of California and Nevada*, 71 pp.

## Midwest

Haga, W. T., *The Sac and Fox Indians*, 1958

Hyde, George, *Indians of the Woodlands*, 1962

Kubiac, William, *Great Lakes Indians: A Pictorial Guide*, 1970

Kinietz, W. V., "Indian Tribes of the Western Great Lakes," *OCMA*, X, 161-225, 1940

Radin, Paul, "The Winnebago Tribe," *ARBAE*, XXXVII, 35-550, 1916

Ritzenthaler, R. E., "The Potawatoni Indians of Wisconsin," *BPMCM*, XIX, 99-174, 1953

Ritzenthaler, R. E., *Woodland Indians of the Western Great Lakes*

Skinner, Alanson, "Material Culture of the Menomini," *INM*, n.s., XX, 1-478, 1921

## Southwest

*Denver Art Museum Leaflet Series*—most of these are on the Southwest

Kluckhohn, Clyde, et al., *Navaho Material Culture*, 1971

Sides, Dorothy S., *Decorative Art of the Southwestern Indians*, 1961

Swanton, John R., *Indian Tribes of the American Southwest*, 1952

Tanner, Clara Lee, *Southwest Indian Craft Arts*, 1968

Waters, Frank, *The Book of the Hopi*, 1963

Young, Robert W., *The Navajo Yearbook*, 1961

## Northwest

Davis, R. T., *Native Arts of the Pacific Northwest*, 1949

Drucker, Philip, *Cultures of the North Pacific Coast*, 1955

Drucker, Philip, *Indians of the Northwest Coast*, 1955

Hawthorne, Audrey, *Art of the Kwakiutl Indians; and Other Northwest Coast Tribes*, 1967

Holm, Bill, *Northwest Coast Indian Art*, 1970

Invararity, R. B., *Art of the Northwest Coast Indians*, 1967

## Indian Attire

Carr, L., "Dress and Ornaments of Certain American Indians," *PAAS*, n.s., XI, pp. 381-454, 1897

Kinietz, Vernon, "Notes on the Roached Headdress of Animal Hair Among the North American Indians," *PMA*, XXVI, pp. 463-67, 1940

Krieger, H. W., "American Indian Costumes in the United States Museum," *ARSI*, pp. 623-61, 1928

Roediger, Virginia M., *Ceremonial Costumes of the Pueblo Indians*, 1941

Wissler, Clark, "Costumes of the Plains Indians," *APAM*, XVII, pp. 39-91

Wissler, Clark, "Indian Costumes of the United States," *AMGLS*, LXIII, pp. 1-32, 1926

Feather Dance, Old-Time Style, Available from Trading Post, and old *AICC*

*CIHA, Costume Outlines*, 21834 Grace Avenue, Carson, CA 90745

## Crafts

Ewers, John C., *Blackfeet Crafts*, 66 pp., 1945

Ewers, John C., "Crow Indian Beadwork," *CMAI*, XVI, 1959

Hunt, William Ben, *Complete Book of Indian Crafts and Lore*, 1958 (To be used for techniques only; newer and more accurate designs and styles are available.)

Hunt, William Ben, and Burshears, J. F., *American Indian Beadwork*, 1951

Lyford, Carrie, *Iroquois Crafts*, 97 pp., 1943

Lyford, Carrie, *Quill and Beadwork of the Western Sioux*, 116 pp., 1962

Mason, Bernard S., *Book of Indian Crafts and Costumes*, 1946

Miller, Preston, *A Manual of Beading Techniques*, 1971

Orchard, W. C., "Beads and Beadwork of the American Indian," *CMAI*, XI, pp. 3-140, 1929

Speck, Frank G., "Notes on the Functional Basis of Decoration and the Feather Techniques of the Oglala Sioux," *INM,* V, pp. 1-41, 1928

Wissler, Clark, "Indian Beadwork," *AMGLS,* V, pp. 1-32, 1946

## Indian Dances

Mason, Bernard S., *Dances and Stories of the American Indians,* 1944

Powers, William, *Here Is Your Hobby: Indian Dancing and Costumes,* 1966

Squires, John L., and McLean, Robert E., *American Indian Dances: Steps, Rhythms, Costumes and Interpretations,* 1963

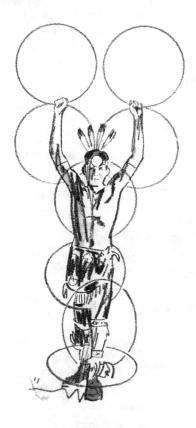

# LENNI-LENAPE WORD LIST

## A

| | |
|---|---|
| Able, One Who is Able | Wunita |
| Abode, residence | Achpineen |
| Accomplished One | Pakantschiechen |
| Active One | Wischixin |
| Advantage, One Who Gives Advantage Unto Others | Ichauweleman |
| Adviser | Witatschimoisin |
| Afoot, He Who Goes Afoot | Pommissin |
| Aged One | Kikey |
| Agreeable One | Nachgundin |
| Agrees, He Who Agrees | Nguttitehen |
| Aids, One Who Aids | Witawematpanni |
| Alder Tree | Topi |
| Alone, One Who is Alone | Nechoha |
| Along the Bank | Japeechen |
| Amusing One | Klakaptonaganall |
| Ant | Elikus |
| Ardent One | Segachtek |
| Arrow | Alluns |
| Assistant | Witawematpanni |
| Assists, One Who Assists | Witschindin |
| Assures, One Who Assures | Kittaptonen |
| Attention, One Who Gets Attention | Papenauwelendam |
| Authority, One Who Has Authority | Tschitanessoagan |
| Away, He Who Goes Away | Elemussit |

## B

| | |
|---|---|
| Babbler, One Who Is A | Wewingtonheet |
| Bachelor | Kikape |
| Back, One Who Comes Back | Apatschin |
| Badger | Gawi |
| Bald Eagle | Woapalanne |
| Bald-Headed One | Moschakantpeu |
| Bear | Machque |
| Bearded One | Tuney |
| Beaver | Ktemaque |
| Bee | Amoe |
| Behaves, He Who Behaves Well | Wulilissin |
| Believer | Olsittam |
| Beloved | Ahotasu |
| Best | Wulit |
| Beyond, He Who Looks Beyond | Wulowachtauwoapin |
| Big | Amangi |
| Big, One Who Is Big And Wide | Elgigunkhaki |
| Birch Tree | Wihhinachk |
| Bird | Awehhelleu |
| Bird, Blackbird | Tskennak |
| Bird, Redbird | Mehokquiman |
| Black | Sukeu |

| | | | |
|---|---|---|---|
| Black Fish | Sukamek | Busy One | Wischiki |
| Black Fox | Wulalowe | Buys, One Who Buys | Ajummen |
| Black Snake | Sukachgook | | |
| Blameless One | Kschiechelensin | Buzzard, Turkey Buzzard | Amatschipuis |
| Blamelessly, He Who Lives Blamelessly | Wawulauchsin | | |

## C

| | | | |
|---|---|---|---|
| Blanket | Akquiwan | | |
| Bleed, One Who Bleeds Fast | Kschiechgochgihillen | Calm-Minded One | Klamhattehamin |
| | | Camper | Mechmauwikenk |
| Blessed One | Welapensit | Canoe, Little Canoe | Amocholes |
| Blue | Schiwapew | | |
| Bluebird | Tschimalus | Capable One | Tschitanissowagan |
| Boat | Amochol | Captain | Lachxowilenno |
| Book | Bambil | Carefree One | Ksinelendam |
| Book Reader | Achgindamen | Careful One | Nechasin |
| Boulder | Ganschapuchk | Cares, One Who Cares | Anatschiton |
| Bow (as in bow and arrow) | Hattape | Carpenter | Gendatehundin |
| Boy | Skahenso | Cat, Wildcat | Nianque |
| Boy, Big Boy | Pilapeu | Cattle Owner | Wdallemunsit |
| Boy, Little Boy | Pilawetit | Cautious One | Anatschihuwewagan |
| Bright | Wachejeu | Cedar, Red Cedar Tree | Mehokhokus |
| Broad | Achgameu | | |
| Brother | Nimat | Cedar, White Cedar Tree | Talala |
| Brother, Elder Brother | Chans | | |
| | | Certain, One Who is Certain | Awelendam |
| Brother, Younger Brother | Chesimus | Chestnut Tree | Woapiminschi |
| | | Chief | Sakima |
| Brotherhood | Wimachtendienk | Chief, Head Chief | Gegeyjumhet |
| Brown | Wipungweu | | |
| Buck (deer) | Ajapeu | Chief, Mighty Chief | Allowat Sakima |
| Buffalo | Sisilija | Child | Amemens |
| Builder | Wikhetschik | Chipmunk | Anicus |
| Bull Frog | Andhanni | Chosen, One | Gegekhuntschik |
| Bullfrog | Oleleu | Clean One | Kschiechek |
| Bushy, a bush | Achewen | Clothing | Ehachquink |
| Business Manager | Nanatschitaquik | Cloud | Achgumhok |

83
←◄

| | | | |
|---|---|---|---|
| Clown | Gebtschaat | **D** | |
| Cold One | Taquatschin | Dancer | Gentgeen |
| Collector | Mawachpo | Day | Gischquik |
| Comes Back, He Who Comes Back | Apatschin | Deep Water | Chitquen |
| | | Deer | Achtu |
| Comforts, One Who Comforts | Wulilaweman | Deer, Young Deer | Mamalis |
| Companion | Nitis | Delights, One Who Delights | Winginamen |
| Comrade | Tschutti | Delivers, One Who Delivers | Nihillasohen |
| Concerned, He Who is Concerned | Lachauweleman | Desires, One Who | Gattamen |
| Confidence, One Who Has Confidence | Nageuchsowagan | Determined One | Gischitehen |
| | | Different One | Tschetschpi |
| Contented One | Tepelendam | Diligent One | Lilchpin |
| Cook | Sachgachtoon | Discerning One | Natenummen |
| Cordial One | Wdehiwi | Doctor | Kikehuwet |
| Counselor | Atschimolsin | Dog | Allum |
| | | Dog, Little Dog | Allumes |
| Counsels, One Who Holds Councils | Witatschimolsin | Door | Esquande |
| | | Doorkeeper | Nutschisquandawet |
| Crane | Taleka | Doubtful One | Quilawelensin |
| Creates, One Who Creates With Hands | Gischihan | Dove | Amimi |
| | | Dove, Wild Dove | Mowichleu |
| Creates, One Who Creates With Mind | Gischeleman | Dreamer | Lungwamen |
| | | Dresses Well, One Who | Wulenensin |
| Cricket | Zelozelos | Drum Beater | Pohonasin |
| Cries, One Who Cries Aloud | Ganschiechsin | **E** | |
| Crow | Ahas | Eagle, Bald Eagle | Woapalanne |
| Cures, One Who Cures | Kikehuwet | Earnest One | Kittlelendamwagan |
| Current, Strong Current | Kschippehellen | Easily, One Who Thinks Easily | Apuelendam |
| Cutter of Wood | Manachewagan | | |

| | |
|---|---|
| East Wind | Achpateuny |
| Easy One | Ksinelendam |
| Eater | Mizin |
| Eight | Chaasch |
| Elder | Kikeyjumhet |
| Elder Brother | Chans |
| Elected One | Gegekhuntschik |
| Elk | Mos |
| Elm Tree | Achgikbi |
| Encourages, One Who Encourages | Gihim |
| Endurance, He Who Has Endurance | Ahowoapewi |
| Endures, He Who Endures Pain | Mamchachwelendam |
| Enjoyable One | Apensuwi |
| Enjoys, One Who Enjoys | Apendamen |
| Enlightens, One Who Enlightens | Gischachsummen |
| Established, One Who is Established | Tschitanigachen |
| Esteemed One | Ahoatam |
| Esteemed, One Who is Highly Esteemed | Allowelendam |
| Excellent One | Wdallowelemuwi |
| Excited One | Glakelendam |
| Exerts, One Who Exerts Himself | Wischixin |
| Exhorts, One Who Exhorts | Guntschitagen |
| Experienced One | Lippoe |
| Extravagant One | Klakelendam |

# F

| | |
|---|---|
| Farmer | Hakihet |
| Farsighted One | Wulowachtauwoapin |
| Fast One | Tschitanek |
| Father, One Who is a Father | Wetochwink |
| Few Times | Keechen |
| Fifth | Palenachtchegit |
| Fighter | Machtagen |
| Fine One | Awullsu |
| Firefly, Lightning Bug | Sasappis |
| Fire Maker | Tindeuchen |
| Fireman | Atenkpatton |
| Firm One | Tschitanigachen |
| First | Netami |
| First Aid, He Who Gives First Aid | Achibis |
| Fish | Names |
| Fish, Large Fish | Amangamek |
| Fisherman | Wendamen |
| Five | Palenach |
| Flies, One Who Flies | Wschimuin |
| Fog, Mist | Awonn |
| Follower | Nosogamen |
| Forceful One | Achtschinkhalan |
| Foremost One | Niganit |
| Forgetful One | Wannessin |
| Foundation | Epigachint |
| Four | Newo |
| Fourth | Neweleneyit |
| Fox, Black Fox | Wulalowe |
| Fox, Gray Fox | Woakus |
| Free One, To Be One's Own Person | Nihillatchi |
| Friend | Elangomat |

| | |
|---|---|
| Friendly-Looking One | Langomuwinaxin |
| Friendly One | Tgauchsin |
| Frog | Tsquall |
| Funny One | Gelackelendam |

# G

| | |
|---|---|
| Gardener | Menhakehhamat |
| Generous One | Wilawilihan |
| Gentle One | Wulamehelleu |
| Giddy One | Gagiwanantpehellan |
| Gives, One Who Gives Back | Guttgennemen |
| Good, He Who Does Good for Others | Wulihan |
| Good One | Awullsu |
| Good-Looking One | Wulinaxin |
| Good-Natured One | Tgauchsin |
| Goose, Wild Goose | Kaak |
| Gracious One | Eluwilissit |
| Grandfather | Muchomes |
| Grasshopper | Kigischgotum |
| Grateful One | Genamuwi |
| Gray | Wipunxit |
| Gray Hair | Woaphokquawon |
| Gray-Headed One | Wapantpeu lenno |
| Great | Macheu |
| Great One | Amangi |
| Great River | Kittan |
| Great Sea | Kittahikan |
| Green | Asgask |
| Groundhog | Gawi |
| Grows, One Who Grows Fast | Lachpikin |

| | |
|---|---|
| Guard | Nutiket |
| Guide | Kichkinet |

# H

| | |
|---|---|
| Hair, Gray Hair | Woaphokquawon |
| Handsome One | Wulisso |
| Half | Pachsiwi |
| Happy, He Who Makes Others Happy | Lauchsoheen |
| Happy One | Wulamallessin |
| Hat, Cap | Allquepi |
| Hawk | Meechgalanne |
| Hawk, Fish Hawk | Nimenees |
| Hawk, Night Hawk | Pischk |
| Hears, One Who Hears Well | Achginchen |
| Heart | Wdee |
| Helpful One | Witscheman |
| Helper | Witschindin |
| Hiker | Achpamsin |
| Hoarse, One Who Is Hoarse | Bihilewen |
| Honest One | Schachachgapewi |
| Honorable One | Wulapeju |
| Honored One | Machelemuxit |
| Hopeful One | Nageuchsin |
| Horse | Nenajunges |
| Horseback Rider | Nenajungeshammen |
| How, One Who Knows How | Wunita |
| Humble One | Gettemagelensit |
| Humility, One Who Has Humility | Tangitehewagan |
| Hungry One | Gattopuin |
| Hunter | Elauwit |

# I

| | |
|---|---|
| Impatient One | Asgalendam |
| Indian Language, One Who Speaks | Helleniechsin |
| Indifferent One | Ajanhelendam |
| Inquiring One | Natoochton |
| Instructs, One Who Instructs | Allohakasin |
| Interpreter | Anhoktonhen |

# J

| | |
|---|---|
| Jocular One | Achgiguwen |
| Journey, One Who Prepares For A Great Journey | Nimawanachen |
| Joyful One | Wulelendam |
| Jumps, One Who Jumps | Laktschehellan |
| Just One | Wulapeju |

# K

| | |
|---|---|
| Kind One | Wulilisseu |
| King, Great King | Kittakima |
| Kinsman | Langoma |
| Knife | Kschikan |
| Knowledge, One Who Has Knowledge | Weuchsowagan |
| Knows, One Who Knows How | Wunita |

# L

| | |
|---|---|
| Lamp | Nendawagan |
| Lamp Carrier | Nendawen |
| Large One | Amangi |
| Laughing One | Gilkissin |
| Leader | Takachsin |
| Lean | Alloku |
| Leisure, One Who Is At | Ksinachpin |
| Left-Handed One | Menantschiwon |
| Life, One Who Gives Life | Lehellechemhaluwet |
| Lifesaver | Gachpallan |
| Lifts, One Who Lifts Up | Aspenummen |
| Listener | Glistam |
| Little One | Tatchen |
| Lively One | Achgiguwen |
| Lives Long, One Who | Segauchsin |
| Lizard | Gegachxis |
| Load, One Who Carries a Load | Najundam |
| Long One | Amiga |
| Looks, One Who Looks Fine | Wulinaxin |
| Loving One | Ahoaltuwl |
| Loyal One | Leke |
| Lucky One | Welapensit |

# M

| | |
|---|---|
| Makes, He Who Makes | Gischihan |
| Man | Lenno |
| Man, Little Man | Lennotit |
| Man, Old Man | Mihillusis |
| Mediator | Etschihillat |
| Medicine Man | Meteu |
| Merchant | Memhallamund |
| Merciful One | Achgettemagelo |
| Merry One | Wulelendam |
| Messenger | Elogamgussit |

| | | | |
|---|---|---|---|
| Mighty and Powerful One | Ehalluchsit | Otter | Gunammochk |
| Mighty One | Allouchsit | Overseer | Genachgihat |
| Mild One | Tgauchsu | Owl | Gokhos |
| Mind, One of Calm Mind | Klamhattenamin | Owl, Little Owl | Gokhotit |

## P

| | |
|---|---|
| Minded, High-Minded One | Machelensin |
| Minister | Pichpemmetonhet |
| Mocking, Jesting | Achgiiki |
| Modest One | Tachpachiwi |
| Mountain | Wachtschu |
| Mouse | Achpoques |
| Mud, Clay | Assisku |
| Muscle, Clam | Ehes |
| Muskrat | Damaskus |

| | |
|---|---|
| Paddle, Oar | Tschimakan |
| Pale One | Woaptigihilleu |
| Panther | Quenischquney |
| Parent | Wenitschanit |
| Part, One Who Takes Part | Apendelluxowagan |
| Partridge | Popokus |
| Patient One | Papesu |
| Pays, One Who Pays | Eenhen |
| Peaceable One | Achwangundowi |
| Peaceful One | Langundowi |

## N

| | |
|---|---|
| Near | Gattati |
| Necessary | Acheweli |
| Neighbor | Pechotschigalit |
| Nephew | Longachsiss |
| Night Hawk | Pischk |
| Nimble One | Wischixin |
| Nine | Peschgonk |
| Noisy One | Achgiguwen |
| North | Lowaneu |
| Nurse | Nechnutschinget |

| | |
|---|---|
| Perplexed One | Ksukquamallsin |
| Persevering One | Tschitanitehen |
| Persuades, One Who Persuades | Achtschinkhalan |
| Physician | Kikehuwet |
| Pigeon | Amemi |
| Pine Tree | Kuwe |
| Pious One | Welilissit |
| Plenty, One Who Has Plenty | Wiaxowagan |
| Poplar Tree | Amocholhe |
| Power, He Who Has Spiritual Power | Mantowagan |
| Powerful, Most Powerful One | Eluwak |
| Powerful One | Allohak |
| Praised, One Who is Praised | Wulakenimgussin |
| Praises, He Who Praises | Amentschinsin |

## O

| | |
|---|---|
| Oak, Black Oak | Wisachgak |
| Oak, White Oak | Wipunquoak |
| Obedient One | Awullsittamuwi |
| Old One | Kikeyin |
| Old Tree | Quetajaku |
| One | Mawat |
| Opossum | Woapink |

| | |
|---|---|
| Preacher | Pichpemmetonhet |
| Prepared, He Who is Prepared | Gischenaxin |
| Pretty One | Awullsu |
| Promise, He Who Keeps a Promise | Wulamoen |
| Proud One | Wulelensin |
| Prudent One | Wewoatamowi |
| Puppy | Allumes |

# Q

| | |
|---|---|
| Quick One | Allapijeyjuwagan |
| Quiet One | Klamachpin |

# R

| | |
|---|---|
| Rabbit | Moskimus |
| Raccoon | Espan |
| Rattlesnake | Wischalowe |
| Reader | Achkindiken |
| Ready, One Who is Ready | Gischhatteu |
| Recommended, One Who is Recommended | Wulakenimgussin |
| Red | Machkeu |
| Redbird | Mehokquiman |
| Redheaded One | Meechgalhukquot |
| Relates, One Who Relates | Atschimolehan |
| Reliable One | Nagatamen |
| Remembers, He Who Remembers | Meschatamen |
| Restless One | Alachimoagan |
| Rests, He Who Rests | Alachimuin |

| | |
|---|---|
| Returns, He Who Returns | Apatschin |
| Rich Man | Pawallessin |
| Righteous One | Schachachgapewi |
| River | Sipo |
| River, One Who Is Along The River, Bank Or Shore | Japeechen |
| Robin | Tschisgokus |
| Rock | Achsin |
| Rock, Big Rock | Ganschapuchk |
| Runner, Fast Runner | Kschamehhellan |

# S

| | |
|---|---|
| Sacrifices, One Who Sacrifices | Wihungen |
| Saddle | Happachpoon |
| Sad One | Sakquelendam |
| Sailor, or Seafarer | Pehachpamhangik |
| Satisfied One | Gispuin |
| Satisfies, One Who Satisfies Others | Eenhawachtin |
| Searches, One Who Searches | Lattoniken |
| Second | Nischeneyit |
| Secretary | Lekhiket |
| Seeker | Elachtoniket |
| Sees, He Who Sees | Nemen |
| Sensitive One | Amandamuwi |
| Sermon | Elittonhink |
| Servant of the Lord | Allogagan Nehellatank |
| Serves, He Who Serves | Allogagan |
| Seven | Nischasch |

| | |
|---|---|
| Sheep | Memekis |
| Shepherd | Nutemekiset |
| Silent One | Tschitgussin |
| Single One | Ngutteleneyachgat |
| Sings, One Who Sings | Nachgohuman |
| Six | Guttasch |
| Skillful One | Wowoatam |
| Small One | Tangetto |
| Snake | Achgook |
| Snow | Guhn |
| Son | Quis |
| Sorrowful One | Uschuwelendam |
| Speaker, Fast Speaker | Lachpiechsin |
| Speaker, Loud Speaker | Amangiechsin |
| Speaks, He Who Speaks Favorably | Wulaptonen |
| Speaks, He Who Speaks Truly | Wulamoc |
| Speaks, One Who Advocates Our Cause | Wulaptonaelchukquonk |
| Speaks Plainly, One Who (or Pronounces Well) | Wuliechsin |
| Spirits, He Who Has Good Spirits | Wulantowagan |
| Spiritual One | Achewon |
| Spiritual, One Who Has Spiritual Power | Mantowagan |
| Spruce Tree | Schind |
| Square One | Haschawije |
| Squirrel, Flying Squirrel | Blaknik |
| Squirrel, Ground Squirrel | Anicus |

| | |
|---|---|
| Squirrel, Red Squirrel | Kuwewanik |
| Star | Allanque |
| Steady One | Clamhattenmoagan |
| Stone | Achsin |
| Stony | Achsinnigeu |
| Stranger | Tschepsit |
| Strengthens, One Who Strengthens | Tschitanissohen |
| Strong One | Achewon |
| Stronger | Tschitami |
| Stubborn One | Amendchewagan |
| Sure One | Bischik |
| Swiftly, He Who Goes Swiftly | Kschihillen |
| Swimmer | Aschowin |

# T

| | |
|---|---|
| Talker | Wewingtonheet |
| Talker, Fast Talker | Alappiechsin |
| Tall One | Gunaquot |
| Teacher | Achgeketum |
| Ten | Metellen |
| Thankful One | Genamuwi |
| There, One Who Is There | Epit |
| Thin One | Waskeu |
| Thinker | Litchen |
| Thinker, Deep Thinker | Achowelendam |
| Thinks, One Who Thinks Easily | Apuelendam |
| Third | Nechit |
| Thoughtful One | Pennauweleman |
| Three | Nacha |
| Tired One | Wiquihillau |
| Toiler | Achowalogen |

| | |
|---|---|
| Torch Carrier | Nendawen |
| Trader | Memhallmund |
| Traveler | Memsochet |
| Traveler, Night Traveler | Nipahwochwen |
| Travels, He Who Travels Alone | Nechochwen |
| Treasurer | Mawachpo |
| Troubled, The Troubled One | Sakquelendamen |
| True, He Who is True | Leke |
| True, He Who Has Proven True | Gischileu |
| Trusted, One Who Can Be Trusted | Nagatamen |
| Trusts, One Who Trusts | Nhakeuchsin |
| Trustworthy One | Nageuchsowagan |
| Truth, Speaker of Truth | Ktschillachton |
| Truthful One | Wulamoewaganit |
| Turkey | Tschikenum |
| Turkey Cock | Bloeu |
| Turtle | Tulpe |
| Twin | Gachpees |
| Two | Nischa |

## U-V

| | |
|---|---|
| Upright One | Wulapejuwagan |
| Useful One | Apensuwi |
| Unconcerned One | Ajanhelendam |
| Understanding One | Pendamen |
| Unlucky One | Palikteminak |
| Valor, Man of Valor | Ilau |

| | |
|---|---|
| Valuable One | Wilawi |
| Violin Player | Achpiquon |
| Visitor | Kiwikaman |

## W-Y-Z

| | |
|---|---|
| Waits, He Who Waits | Pesoop |
| Walker | Pemsit |
| Walker, Fast Walker | Kschochwen |
| Walks, He Who Walks Alone | Nechochwen |
| Warrior | Netopalis |
| Wasp | Amoe |
| Watchman | Wewoapisak |
| Water | Mbi |
| Water, Clear Water | Kschiechpecat |
| Water, Deep Water | Chuppecat |
| Water, Still Water | Klampeechen |
| Weasel | Sanquen |
| Well Behaved | Welauchsit |
| Well, He Who is Always Well | Wawulamallessin |
| West | Wundchenneu |
| Whippoorwill | Quekolis |
| White | Wapsu |
| Wide One | Achgameu |
| Willful | Ahoweli |
| Willing One | Nuwingi |
| Wind, East Wind | Achpateuny |
| Wind, West Wind | Linchen |
| Winner | Wsihuwen |
| Wise One | Lippoe |
| Wiseman | Wowoatammowino |

| | | | |
|---|---|---|---|
| Witty One | Luppoewagan | Worker, Hard Worker | Achowalogen |
| Wolf | Wiechcheu | Worthy One | Elgixin |
| Wonderful One | Wulelemi | Wounded One | Achpequot |
| Wonders, One Who Does Great Wonders | Ganschelalogen | Writer | Lekhiket |
| | | Yellow | Wisaweu |
| Wood Gatherer | Natachtu | Younger Brother | Chesimus |
| Woodcock | Memeu | Zealous One | Skattek |
| Woodcutter | Giskhaquen | | |
| Woodpecker | Papaches | | |
| Work, One Who Does Good Work | Wulalogewagan | | |

# INDEX